ABOUT ISLAND PRESS

Island Press, a nonprofit organization, publishes, markets, and distributes the most advanced thinking on the conservation of our natural resources—books about soil, land, water, forests, wildlife, and hazardous and toxic wastes. These books are practical tools used by public officials, business and industry leaders, natural resource managers, and concerned citizens working to solve both local and global resource problems.

Founded in 1978, Island Press reorganized in 1984 to meet the increasing demand for substantive books on all resource-related issues. Island Press publishes and distributes under its own imprint and offers these services to other nonprofit organizations.

Support for Island Press is provided by Apple Computers, Inc., Mary Reynolds Babcock Foundation, Geraldine R. Dodge Foundation, The Educational Foundation of America, The Charles Engelhard Foundation, The Ford Foundation, Glen Eagles Foundation, The George Gund Foundation, William and Flora Hewlett Foundation, The Joyce Foundation, The J. M. Kaplan Fund, The John D. and Catherine T. MacArthur Foundation, The Andrew W. Mellon Foundation, The Joyce Mertz-Gilmore Foundation, The New-Land Foundation, The Jessie Smith Noyes Foundation, The J. N. Pew, Jr. Charitable Trust, Alida Rockefeller, The Rockefeller Brothers Fund, The Florence and John Schumann Foundation, The Tides Foundation, and individual donors.

ABOUT THE RURAL ECONOMIC POLICY PROGRAM OF THE ASPEN INSTITUTE

The Rural Economic Policy Program (REPP) was created in 1985 as a collaborative program of The Aspen Institute, The Ford Foundation, and the Wye Institute. Working closely with The Ford Foundation's Rural Poverty and Resources Program, the REPP encourages greater attention to rural policy issues through a program of research grants, seminars, and public education. The Program is focused on rural concerns, including agricultural policy, community economic development, resource management, and enhanced livelihoods for the rural poor. REPP is funded by a grant from The Ford Foundation.

The Rural Economic Policy Program is housed at The Aspen Institute in Washington, D.C. The Aspen Institute is an international nonprofit organization whose broad purpose is to seek consideration of human values in areas of leadership development and public policy formulation. Since its founding in 1949, The Aspen Institute has operated a program of Executive Seminars in which leaders of business, government, the arts, education, law, and the media convene with distinguished scholars to reinforce the application of traditional humanistic values in their personal and professional deliberations. The Aspen Institute's Policy Programs, one of which is the Rural Economic Policy Program, seek to advance the formulation of public policy in areas of communications and information technology; the environment; political, economic, and strategic issues for the U.S. in its relations with other nations; and education. The Aspen Institute also operates a set of international programs and activities, principally in Europe and the Pacific Rim.

A
COMMUNITY
RESEARCHER'S
GUIDE TO
RURAL DATA

A COMMUNITY RESEARCHER'S GUIDE TO RURAL DATA

by Priscilla Salant

RURAL ECONOMIC POLICY PROGRAM
OF THE ASPEN INSTITUTE

ISLAND PRESS

Washington, D.C. □ *Covelo, California*

Library of Congress Cataloging-in-Publication Data

Salant, Priscilla.
  A community researcher's guide to rural data / Priscilla Salant.
    p.   cm.
  Includes bibliographical references.
  ISBN 1-55963-047-7. — ISBN 1-55963-046-9 (pbk.)
  1. United States—Population, Rural—Statistical services.
2. United States—Rural conditions—Statistics. 3. Community development—United States. 4. Rural development—United States.
I. Title.
HB2385.S25   1990
330.973'009173'4—dc20   90–31780
                                                          CIP

Printed on recycled, acid-free paper

Manufactured in the United States of America
10 9 8 7 6 5 4 3 2 1

ACKNOWLEDGMENTS

This manual was funded by a grant from the Rural Poverty and Resources Program of The Ford Foundation with assistance from the Rural Economic Policy Program of The Aspen Institute. The author gratefully acknowledges generous support and patience from Norman Collins at The Ford Foundation and Susan Sechler at The Aspen Institute.

The author would also like to thank the people who provided thoughtful comments and suggestions on earlier drafts of the manuscript. They include Peggy Adams, Paul Barkley, Henry Carey, Annabel Cook, Ron Faas, Peggy Ross, Richard Salant, Barbara Smith, Marty Strange, and Kathryn Wallman.

Special appreciation goes to Tracy Huston, Phil Halverson, and Danny Wright for helping with the logistics of preparing this publication. Their patience and attention to detail made the final draft a reality.

Last, the author would like to thank two individuals who provided much of the inspiration for this work, Cynthia Duncan and Jim Bonnen.

TABLE OF CONTENTS

LIST OF TABLES

LIST OF FIGURES

INTRODUCTION

This manual was prepared at the request of the Rural Economic Policy Program of The Aspen Institute, and supported with funds from The Ford Foundation. Staff from both organizations recognize that reliable and timely data are a prerequisite for sound planning and policy development. Unfortunately, decision makers in rural communities are often hampered in their work because they don't know that such data exist or where to find them.

Hence, the purpose of this manual is to acquaint researchers with data that they can use to describe and better understand rural communities. The manual is intended primarily for researchers in locally based community development organizations, although researchers and other analysts in universities, state governments, and policy institutes will also find it useful.

For those who are interested in why this manual was written, a historical context and justification are provided in the next section. The chapter concludes with an explanation of how the manual is organized.

Background

Rural America has experienced dramatic demographic and economic changes in the last several decades. During the 1960s and 1970s, population and employment in rural communities grew, and the long-standing gap between rural and urban incomes became smaller. Just when many analysts were predicting an economic revival in rural America, the fortunes turned. The income gap began to grow again and migration from rural to urban areas resumed.

Since the early 1980s, several factors have combined to worsen economic conditions in rural communities. International forces (such as global competition), structural change in the U.S. economy (with significant job losses in goods production), and deregulation (particularly in the transportation and credit industries) have left few rural communities untouched.

Adjusting to change of this magnitude is an enormous challenge. Public and private decision makers at all levels face the task of building a more resilient, diversified rural economy—and that task requires reliable information and analysis.

Many analysts argue that data collection and research on rural communities have not kept pace with changing conditions. Part of the reason for the gaps in our knowledge is obvious—the cost of collecting reliable statistical data increases in less populated areas. Most national data collection efforts utilize sample designs that yield enough observations to make estimates with relatively small sampling errors for urban populations, but not for rural populations. The result is that researchers often lack accurate and timely data to describe conditions in rural communities.

In their 1981 report, *Rural America in Passage*, a panel convened by the National Research Council (NRC) broke new ground by comprehensively documenting what analysts *cannot say and do not know* about rural communities (20).[1] The panel concluded that current reporting practices for rural data are seriously misleading because they impose an artificial division between rural and urban areas, as if every community in America could be classified as one or the other polar extreme. Instead of this division or dichotomy framework that obscures a tremendously diverse rural America, analysts and policy makers would be better served by information from a continuum between the most remote and the most accessible rural communities. A reporting system that accommodated such a continuum would provide a more precise language to describe rural communities.[2]

The NRC panel also concluded that researchers and policy makers lack an understanding of nonagricultural economic activities and of disadvantaged populations in rural America—a shortcoming due to inadequate data as well as to research priorities. More recently, participants in a symposium sponsored by the Congressional Research Service and the Joint Economic Committee of Congress argued that researchers need to pay careful attention to three additional subjects—work and income distribution; long-term economic and social trends; and intensive, qualitative analyses that test our perceptions and deepen our understanding of conditions in rural America (11).

These national panels have focused attention on where our research and statistical programs should be heading. But just as important as documenting what we *cannot* say about rural communities is documenting what we *can* say. Although policy changes and budget cuts have, in the view of many social scientists, seriously weakened the Federal statistical system,[3] a wealth of secondary data still exists. This manual identifies these data sources for both experienced researchers and local decision makers who are unfamiliar with statistical data.

In the context of identifying data sources, "rural" is a geographic concept based on two standards defined by Federal agencies that collect statistics. The first is the urban/rural designation used by the Bureau of the Census in its decennial count of population and housing units. An *urban* area is any incorporated or unincorporated place with a population of at least 2,500, and *rural* is any place not classified as urban. A few other Federal agencies that collect data report statistics for rural and urban areas. Unfortunately, not many are mandated to draw samples that are large enough to describe the rural population in detail.

The second standard is the metropolitan designation assigned to every county by the U.S. Office of Management and Budget. *Metropolitan* counties include cities and their satellite communities. *Nonmetropolitan* counties, which numbered 2,383 according to the last "complete count" Census figures (1980), are all others, that is, a *residual*. Because the county unit is the building block of the vast majority of Federal data sources, nonmetro counties become the building blocks of rural data systems, if only by default.[4]

At present, we can make two refinements to the nonmetro county designation. Both are based on classification systems developed by the USDA's Economic Research Service (ERS). The first, often referred to as the Beale coding system, classifies six groups of nonmetro counties based on how urban (or rural) their population is and on how close they are to metro areas. At one end of the spectrum are "urbanized adjacent" counties that have an urbanized population of at least 20,000 and are adjacent to a metro area. At the other end are "totally rural nonadjacent" counties that have no urban population (that is, no place with a population of at least 2,500) and are not adjacent to a metro area.[5]

The second refinement we can make to nonmetro county designations is to use the Policy Impact (or ERS "county-type") coding system which classifies nonmetro counties according to their economic base, the presence of federally owned land, and population characteristics (including retirement and persistently poor). ERS developed these codes to help policy makers and researchers understand the diversity of social and economic conditions in nonmetro areas.[6]

With these refinements to commonly used statistical reporting practices, we can at least begin to describe rural America. The centerpiece of our information base is the Decennial Census of Population and Housing that is conducted by the Department of Commerce every ten years. Using this rich data file, we can describe *in detail* the demographic and economic characteristics of small area populations. For example, the decennial census allows us to answer questions about work and income distribution, educational attainment, and the economic well-being of particular types of households.

In between the decennial censuses, we supplement our knowledge about rural America with a variety of less comprehensive sources. A few examples make the point. Estimates from a joint Federal/state program give us a rough idea of population change in small areas from year to year. (County estimates are produced annually and subcounty estimates are produced biannually.) The economic censuses that are conducted every 5 years permit us to describe the structure and activity of the most important industries in each county in the U.S. (albeit with few details). The Bureau of Economic Analysis estimates annual county-level per capita and total personal income and its components. And, data from the Department of Health and Human Services describes the health resources and status of county populations.

Who needs this kind of data? People who make decisions about where rural communities are heading. Public and private community development practitioners, university researchers, elected officials, and policy makers from the local to the federal level all use data and information about rural communities. The purpose of this manual is to help them find what they need.

Organization of the Manual

Chapter 1 of this guide describes a few basic concepts for readers who are not experienced data users. The topics discussed are: primary vs. secondary data; census vs. administrative data; sample vs. population surveys; the media in which data are available; and census geography.

Chapter 2 provides an overview of major data sources that can be used to describe rural communities, including the Census Bureau's decennial and current population programs; the Census Bureau's agricultural, economic, and government censuses; personal income data from the Bureau of Economic Analysis; and labor market data from the Bureau of Labor Statistics. Chapter 3 concludes by explaining where researchers can find data that are generated by these agencies.

Chapters 3, 4, and 5 show how researchers can use Federal, state, and local data to understand social and economic change in the very diverse communities that make up rural America. Sample counties from six of ERS's Policy Impact groups (see page 2) are used to put our data sources in context.[7] This classification scheme enables us to show how various data sources can be used to explore major rural issues, including the performance of critical economic sectors, the aging of the population, local government, and poverty.

The sample counties are:

- Attala County, Mississippi, a "persistent poverty" county;
- Burnet County, Texas, a "retirement" county;
- Coos County, New Hampshire, a "manufacturing-dependent" county;
- Kossuth County, Iowa, a "farming-dependent" county;
- Nicholas County, West Virginia, a "mining-dependent" county; and
- Whitman County, Washington, a "specialized government" county.

The appendices provide readers with addresses and phone numbers for state and Federal offices that house or collect data; details about Census Bureau publications and economic census programs; and information on how to use the Bureau of the Census' *County and City Data Book* in diskette form.

A glossary at the end of the manual gives precise definitions of research and statistical terms and finally, a reference table on the inside back cover explains acronyms used in the text.

Three comments before we begin—first, most of this manual concerns data reported by Federal agencies. However, researchers who are interested primarily in local conditions may find more up-to-date and detailed data from state and private sources (such as local employers). These researchers are encouraged to pursue contacts in their own communities, as well as state resources. (See Appendix D.)

Second, knowing where to find reliable data is one important part of research. Another is interpreting and analyzing data to provide information for decision making (6). To find out what kind of analysis has been done on rural communities in your state or region, contact either your state land grant university or regional rural development center. (There are four regional centers around the country—see Appendix C.)

Another useful contact is the Rural Information Center (RIC) at the National Agricultural Library. The RIC provides information and referral services to local officials, community development professionals, and private citizens. RIC staff responds to inquiries on topics such as current USDA research, Cooperative Extension Service programs, and economic development funding sources. They also conduct database searches and help people use the National Agricultural Library collection. You can contact the RIC through your county or state Extension office, by telephone (301/344-2547), or by mail (RIC, National Agricultural Library, Room 304, Beltsville, Maryland 20705).

Finally, two caveats about using the data described here: first, the value of most data lies not with a single statistic for one particular area, but in comparable statistics for different areas or different time periods. For example, an indivudual county's unemployment rate is more telling when compared to the rate in surrounding counties because it is put in a *relative context*. Our statistical indicators are too imprecise to contain "absolute truth" by themselves.

Second, statistics are only as valuable as the questions people ask. The most carefully collected data are useless if researchers have not asked questions whose answers inform us about issues that matter. To emphasize that good research begins with good questions, data in this manual are described in the context of how they can be used. It is hoped that the illustrative questions we pose will encourage more substantive and informative research on rural communities.

The Sample Counties[8]

Attala County, Mississippi: a persistent poverty county . . . where per capita personal income was in the lowest quintile in each of the years 1950, 1959, 1969, and 1979.

In 1985, ten percent of all nonmetro counties were classified as persistent poverty counties—they contained about 6 percent of the nonmetro population. Nine out of 10 of these counties are in Appalachia, the Ozark-Ouachita Plateau, and the Mississippi Delta.

Compared to others who live in nonmetro counties, people in persistent poverty counties are less likely to have completed high school, and more likely to have a work-limiting disability, to be black, and to be underemployed.

Encouraging development is especially difficult in persistent poverty counties. One reason is that their public services (such as education) are not well-developed. Research clearly indicates that poverty is much more common among people with less education. Hence, a key issue facing counties like Attala is how to remedy deficiencies in education and basic skills and how to overcome problems that prevent people from participating in the labor force.

Burnet County, Texas: a retirement county . . . where net in-migration rates of people aged 60 and over were 15 percent or more of the expected 1980 population aged 60 and over in the period 1970–1980.

In 1985, just over one-fifth of all nonmetro counties were classified as retirement counties—they contained about one-fourth of the nonmetro population. Retirement counties tend to be located in remote (and often scenic) rural areas—they are scattered around the country with the largest concentrations in eastern Texas and the Ozarks, in Florida, parts of the Upper Great Lakes states, and in several western states.

In recent years, the population in retirement counties has grown more rapidly than in most other nonmetro counties. Their growth is due not only to elderly in-migrants, but also to working age people who are attracted by job opportunities. Transfer payments (like Social Security) are an important source of income to people in these counties. Earnings from trade and services are also important, although wage rates in these industries tend to be relatively low.

Important issues in counties like Burnet concern the availability and cost of providing services (including health care) to the growing elderly population, and in some areas, problems associated with rapid growth.

Coos County, New Hampshire: a manufacturing-dependent county . . . where manufacturing contributed at least 30 percent of total labor and proprietor income in 1979.

In 1985, 28 percent of all nonmetro counties were classified as manufacturing-dependent—they contained 39 percent of the nonmetro population. Manufacturing counties tend to be more urbanized than other nonmetro counties and are more likely to be adjacent to a metropolitan area. Over half are in the Southeast; others are concentrated in the North Central region and, to a lesser extent, in the Northwest and Northeast.

The rural manufacturing sector is diverse—some regions specialize in natural resource-based manufacturing (like lumber and wood products in Coos County); others specialize in routine manufacturing that relies mainly on assembly-line skills (like textiles); and still others concentrate on complex manufacturing that relies on technically skilled labor. Each type of manufacturing is vulnerable to different competitive pressures. Routine manufacturers, for example, are especially vulnerable to competition from countries where labor is relatively cheap. An important issue facing such counties is how to upgrade the local labor force through education and job training.

Kossuth County, Iowa: a farming-dependent county . . . where farming contributed a weighted annual average of at least 20 percent of total labor and proprietor income over the five years from 1975 to 1979.

In 1985, 29 percent of all nonmetro counties were classified as farming-dependent—they contained about 13 percent of the nonmetro population. These counties tend to be remote—they are concentrated in the North Central region and are also scattered along the Mississippi River Delta, in parts of the Southeast, and in Idaho, Montana, and Washington.

On average, population in farming-dependent counties fell during the 1960s, increased slowly in the 1970s, and in recent years, has begun to decline again (probably in response to financial stress in the agricultural sector). These counties tend to have a higher percentage of people aged 65 and over than other nonmetro counties (except retirement counties). Per capita personal income tends to be relatively high, although income is less evenly distributed among the population.

One of the most important issues facing counties like Kossuth is the shape of Federal agricultural policies, especially those that affect net farm income. Other key issues are the out-migration of young people, the lack of off-farm job opportunities, and the environmental effects of current agricultural practices.

Nicholas County, West Virginia: a mining-dependent county . . . where mining contributed 20 percent or more to total labor and proprietor income in 1979.

In 1985, eight percent of all nonmetro counties were classified as mining-dependent—they contained six percent of the nonmetro population. Mining-dependent counties are concentrated in the coal-producing areas of Appalachia and the Midwest; the oil-producing areas of Texas, Oklahoma, and the Louisiana gulf coast; and throughout the Southwest and West.

Mining counties are vulnerable to intense foreign and domestic competition as well as to shifts in the demand for energy and mineral resources. As a result, income and employment in counties like Nicholas are relatively unstable and one of the most important issues they face is how to provide stable economic development that benefits the whole community.

Whitman County, Washington: a specialized government county . . . where Federal, state, and local government activities contributed 25 percent or more to total labor and proprietor income in 1979.

Specialized government counties (which made up 13 percent of all nonmetro counties in 1985) are scattered around the country. In recent years, the population in government counties has increased faster than in most nonmetro counties, probably because of employment opportunities generated by government spending. Paradoxically, however, both per capita personal income and the proportion of the population employed have been lower, on average, than in other nonmetro counties.

Government activities that generate income in these counties include military bases, public parks and forests, universities and colleges (as in Whitman County), State capitals, and prisons. Each activity is associated with different population and labor force characteristics, as well as with different support services. In addition, counties like Whitman tend to have more diverse economies than most nonmetro counties. Despite this diversity, their reliance on government activities makes this group of counties particularly susceptible to policy decisions about the geographic distribution and level of public spending.

Notes

1. Underlined numbers in parentheses refer to sources listed in the Reference section of this report beginning on page 67.
2. As Bonnen suggests, we lack a satisfactory reporting system because we have not developed a conceptual framework to define what is meant by the term "rural" (6). Absent a conceptual framework, researchers let existing data define the concept by default.
3. See, for example, Wallman, Katherine K., *Losing Count: The Federal Statistical System,* (61) and Bonnen, James T., "The Statistical Data Base for Rural America," (7).
4. In rare cases, we have data for sub-county areas such as municipalities. These data are generally only available from economic and population censuses.

5. The Beale coding system also classifies four groups of metro counties. Codes for all counties in the United States are available on diskette for $25 from "ERS Data," Room 228, 1301 New York Avenue NW, Washington D.C. 20005-4788.
6. ERS is revising this system. The original codes are available from "ERS Data" for $25. See footnote 5.
7. The classification system used here is adopted from Bender et al., "The Diverse Social and Economic Structure of Nonmetropolitan America," (3).
8. This section is based on Bender et al., (3). See the original publication for precise classification criteria and for maps that show where counties in each group are located.

DATA CONCEPTS

data . . . things known or assumed; facts or figures from which conclusions can be inferred; information (13)

statistics . . . facts or data of a numerical kind, assembled, classified, and tabulated so as to present significant information about a given subject (13)

Kinds of Data

From the researcher's perspective, statistical data come from either primary or secondary sources. Primary data are those collected directly by the researcher for a specific study using, for example, personal or telephone interviews. Secondary sources are existing data (collected by a government institution or private vendor) that the researcher uses for his or her particular analysis. This manual is solely concerned with secondary data sources. To the extent that researchers find secondary sources inadequate (whether because of detail, accuracy, or timeliness), they may wish to collect primary data.

Secondary data have been collected in either census or survey form (U.S. Bureau of the Census) or administratively, in the course of an organization's normal business (Internal Revenue Service or Social Security Administration). Both survey and administrative data are discussed in this manual.

How Data are Available

Statistical data are issued in two principal media:

- *Hard copy* (either in a publication, on a computer printout, or on microfiche); and

- *Electronic format*, that is, computer accessible (either on tape, diskette, laser disc, or "on-line").

Computer printouts and published statistical data require no special equipment to use and are the most readily available through local libraries and agencies. However, they are also the bulkiest and often do not contain as much detail as other forms of data, nor are they regularly reissued when data are revised. Further, data in this form must be manipulated or "recombined" by hand. Researchers can request a computer printout of specific tabulations from some government and private agencies when they know exactly what statistics they need and are willing to pay the extra cost.

Microfiche—hard copy in "mini-form"—are 4 x 6 inch sheets of microfilm containing from 98 to 420 images arranged in a grid. Microfiche can be viewed with machine readers which are readily available in local libraries. Microfiche are inexpensive to purchase and distribute by mail (because they take up little space and are lightweight). All printed reports from the 1970 Census are contained on 4,352 microfiche, which take up less than one cubic foot of shelf space (18).

Computer accessible data—data in electronic format that can be read and manipulated by a computer—require either a mainframe (for tapes) or a personal computer (for diskettes and laser discs). Tape files, such as those produced by the U.S. Bureau of the Census, may be highly detailed and require some programming expertise to use.

As personal computers gain in popularity, data on diskettes are becoming more widely available and generally come with utility software that make them "user friendly." In addition, more software is being written to meet the needs of less specialized users.

"On-line" data files are those which are stored in a computer and can be accessed by computer users with a modem (which translates signals between a computer and a telephone).[1] Most on-line files consist of bibliographic information, although a limited amount of statistical data are also available.

CD-ROMs—laser compact discs with "read only memory"—can be used on personal computers with the proper hardware and software. They are likely to be used widely in the future because of their enormous data storage capability. Each can hold as much as four magnetic tapes at 6,250 bits per inch or 1,600 flexible diskettes.

This manual focuses on data that are issued in hard copy and diskette form. Almost all of these data are also issued on tapes or CD-ROM. Researchers should contact the issuing agency if they have the necessary hardware and expertise to use tape and CD-ROM files.

Population vs. Sample Data

Each decade since 1790, the U.S. Census Bureau has conducted a population *census*. A census is a count, or enumeration, of the total population in a given area. Censuses can include things other than people—since 1940, the U.S. Census has also enumerated housing units.

Planning for the 1990 decennial census began in 1983; its total cost will be roughly $2.6 billion. By mid-1990, the Bureau will employ about 400,000 temporary workers in addition to its regular staff. When the 1990 Census population reports are all issued by 1993, data will be available for areas as small as single blocks (24).

Contrast the decennial census with the Census Bureau's Current Population Survey (CPS), which is a *monthly* survey that gathers data from a *sample* of the population—about 60,000 households. A sample is "part" of a population carefully selected to represent the "whole" population. The Census Bureau and the Bureau of Labor Statistics (BLS) use the CPS sample to estimate many widely quoted statistics, including the unemployment rate and the percentage of persons with incomes below the poverty level.

The kind of data collected in the CPS is similar to that in the decennial census, but because it comes from a *sample*, it cannot be used to analyze areas below the regional (and in some cases, the state) level. Estimates about smaller geographic areas are unreliable because of the relatively small sample size—the smaller the sample, the greater the margin of error.

Sampling is critical to research. By scientifically choosing a sample of observations that represents an entire population, researchers save money and time on data collection and analysis. They survey fewer people, and they process less data.[2]

To illustrate this point, consider the case of poverty estimates from the Bureau of the Census. Using only CPS data from the 60,000-household sample, the Bureau estimates the number of persons and families with incomes below the poverty level for the nation as a whole, for regions of the country (South and Nonsouth), and for certain demographic groups (like female-headed households in nonmetro areas). The Federal government gets the statistics it needs (and saves money) by surveying only a representative sample of 60,000 households in between the decennial census years.[3]

Many of the data sources described in this manual are derived from samples of a population rather than censuses. The detail and accuracy of estimates based on samples depend on how large the sample size is as well as on how similar the sample is to the population. A larger sample yields greater accuracy, that is, a smaller *margin of error*.

Census Geography and the Notion of Rural[4]

The U.S. Bureau of the Census, which produces much of the data discussed in this manual, reports statistics for geographical areas ranging from the entire United States to single city blocks. Some of the areas are governmental units (legally defined areas such as states and counties), while others are defined by the Census Bureau solely for purposes of collecting data (such as regions and "enumeration districts"). Understanding Census Bureau geography is an important part of making the most effective use of the agency's data.

Figure 1 illustrates the four census regions defined for the United States. They include the West, Midwest, Northeast, and South. Each region is composed of two or more geographic divisions or groupings of states. The states themselves consist of counties and their equivalents (3,137 plus 78 in Puerto Rico).

Figure 2 shows the national geographic relationships used by the Census Bureau. Counties are divided into either (1) minor civil divisions (MCDs), which are town and township governmental units (about 25,000 total), or (2) census county divisions (CCDs). CCDs are statistical units designated by the Census Bureau in states where MCDs do not exist. They total 5,512 (plus 37 boroughs in Alaska).

In addition to being divided into counties (and MCDs and CCDs), states are also broken down into (1) incorporated places, which are governmental designations, and (2) census designated

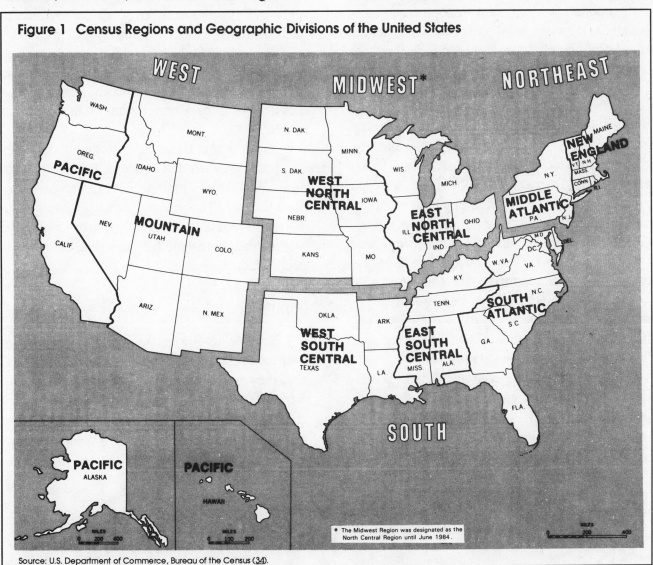

Figure 1 Census Regions and Geographic Divisions of the United States

* The Midwest Region was designated as the North Central Region until June 1984.

Source: U.S. Department of Commerce, Bureau of the Census (34).

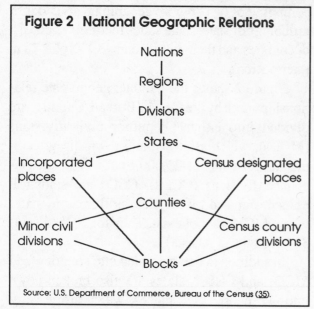

Figure 2 National Geographic Relations

Nations

Regions

Divisions

States

Incorporated places   Census designated places

Counties

Minor civil divisions   Census county divisions

Blocks

Source: U.S. Department of Commerce, Bureau of the Census (35).

places (CDPs), which are unincorporated, closely settled population centers with populations of at least 1,000. Incorporated places and CDPs sometimes cross county boundaries and are therefore shown separately from the county hierarchy in Figure 2.

In the past, MCDs and CCDs were further divided into either enumeration districts (primarily in rural areas) or block groups.[5] Unfortunately, this system made legislative redistricting difficult for the states. Districts and block groups were too large for precise, small area population counts, and furthermore, their boundaries did not always coincide with voting districts. To remedy these problems, the Census Bureau will divide all MCDs and CCDs into blocks for the 1990 Census. In rural areas, block boundaries may be visible features such as roads, powerlines, and shorelines. They may also include features such as fences, canyons and ravines, and abandoned railroads.

The Census Bureau uses two other classification schemes that are pertinent to rural data use. The first classifies the entire U.S. population into either metropolitan or nonmetropolitan. The Office of Management and Budget has desig-

nated some 285 metropolitan statistical areas (MSAs). MSAs are made up of one or more counties around a large population center together with adjacent communities which are socially and economically integrated with the central city. (Integration is measured in terms of the number of workers who commute to the central county).[6] MSAs are made up of entire counties to make gathering and comparing data easier. People who live in metropolitan counties comprise the *metro* population, while everyone else makes up the *nonmetro* population. In the early 1980s, OMB classified 2,383 counties (and selected independent cities) as nonmetro. These counties are indicated in Figure 3.

The final scheme, illustrated in Figure 4, breaks the total population into either urban or rural. All persons living in urbanized areas (defined as central cities and surrounding densely settled territory with a combined population of at least 50,000) as well as those living in places of 2,500 outside urban areas are classified as urban. The rest of the population is considered rural (either farm or nonfarm).

The urban/rural and metro/nonmetro schemes are based on different concepts so they are not interchangeable, although many researchers confuse the two. The urban/rural split actually cuts across the metro/nonmetro split—urban areas exist within nonmetro counties and rural areas exist within metro counties.

Public vs. Private Data

The Census Bureau and other Federal, state, and local agencies are *public* data sources. The data they estimate or collect are produced at public expense in order to carry out some statutorily initiated program or regulation. They make data available to the public on a cost recovery basis or free of charge, as a pubic service.

For the first time, the entire U.S. has been blocked for the 1990 Census.
The first block-level statistics to be released are total population counts, distribution by race, and percentage of Hispanic population. These data will be made available to all State Data Centers by April 1991. Other block-level statistics will be issued later on microfiche and CD-ROM.

Figure 3   Nonmetropolitan Counties

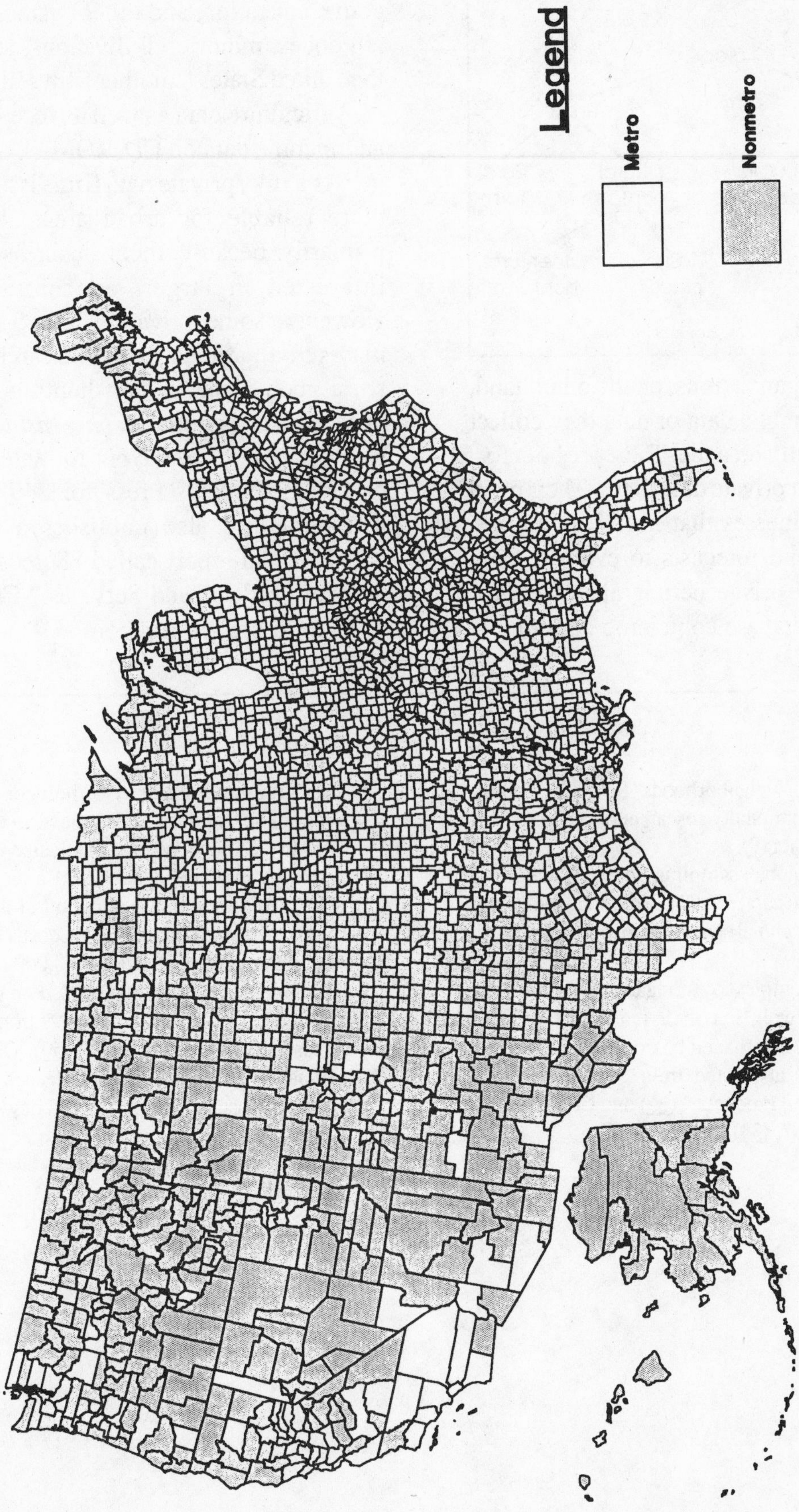

Legend

Metro

Nonmetro

Source: Economic Research Service, USDA

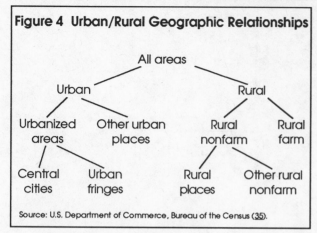

Figure 4 Urban/Rural Geographic Relationships

Source: U.S. Department of Commerce, Bureau of the Census (35).

Private data organizations, on the other hand, offer repackaged public data or data they collect themselves, generally for a fee. There are both for-profit and nonprofit private data firms. Their main customers are businesses that need easy-to-use, current statistics and forecasts to evaluate consumer markets. One private demographic firm, for example, sells a database containing current and projected population estimates by age, sex, income, education, and other characteristics for all zip codes, minor civil divisions, and counties in the United States. Another firm sells 1987 Census of Agriculture data as well as recent employment and income data on CD-ROM.

As a rule, private data firms issue data that are more reliable for urban areas than for rural, primarily because their business clientele are interested in larger, concentrated markets. However, some privately issued data products may suit a particular rural researcher's needs. If so, a good place to start hunting for a suitable private data vendor is *The Insider's Guide to Demographic Know-How* for sale from American Demographics Press for $49.95. American Demographics also publishes a regularly updated special report called "Directory of Demographic Products and Services." Call (800) 828-1133 for more information.

Notes

1. See "Computers for Neighborhoods" for more information about how community researchers can use computer accessible data (9).
2. For a good discussion of sampling, see *The Practice of Social Research*, Chapter 7, (2). Note that some data collected in the decennial census are also sample based. See page 17.
3. Researchers use samples to estimate poverty rates for smaller areas as well, but their margin of error is necessarily larger. See shaded box on page 37.
4. This discussion is abstracted from "Census Geography—Concepts and Products," (35) and *Census Catalog and Guide 1987*, (34).

5. The definition of a block is a "polygon with discernable geographic features." Blocks have *no minimum population*. In 1980, the average block size was 72 people.
6. An MSA must either have: (a) a city (i.e., an incorporated place) with a population of at least 50,000 or (b) an urbanized area (i.e., a Census designated area) with a population of at least 50,000 *and* a total MSA population of at least 100,000. For the precise definition, see "New Standards for Metropolitan Statistical Areas," in *Data User News*, (50). OMB reviews the official MSA definition each decade prior to the decennial census. Hence, the agency may revise the definition soon.

CHAPTER 2

OVERVIEW OF SOURCES

The core of our knowledge about rural communities comes from the Census of Population and Housing that the Federal government conducts every ten years. We supplement these decennial census data with other statistics from the Bureau of the Census as well as with information from a variety of other Federal, state and local agencies (Figure 5).

The section below describes the most important sources of data that researchers can use to analyze rural communities. The chapter closes with a description of several useful reference materials and statistical compendia.

The Decennial Census of Population and Housing

The Census Bureau is the Federal agency that is primarily responsible for collecting and publishing information about individuals, households, businesses, and governments. Foremost among the agency's activities is the decennial census, which is an invaluable source of information for two reasons. First, it is exceptionally rich in the detail it provides, and second, it is *nationally uniform* for all geographic areas. In fact, the decennial census is our only nationally uniform, small-area source of data for such important variables as educational attainment, poverty rates, and employment by occupation. (Local organizations, businesses, or units of government may conduct surveys or develop methods to estimate such variables from secondary data sources, but their information *cannot be compared* to other areas in the country.)

Tips for Community Researchers: How to Locate and Use Data

• *Find a well-informed, helpful reference librarian who can assist you in tracking down documents, phone numbers, and personal contacts.* Try your public library first, but if help is unavailable, go to the library at the nearest community college.

• *If no one in your community can help you find the data you need, call the source.* Keep calling until you get what you need. Reference books like those discussed on pages 24–26 of this report are designed to help you find people to call.

• *Read the technical documentation that accompanies each of your data sources.* This material explains how the data were collected and provides definitions of terms used in the document. It may be helpful to review the questionnaire that was used to collect the data. Many agencies include a copy in the appendix of their publications.

• *Be precise in your use of research terms.* Make sure you understand the definitions of terms you use to describe the characteristics of your community, such as *labor force, unemployment rate,* and *poverty level.* Refer to the Glossary at the end of this report, as well as the data sources that you use.

15

Figure 5   Major Sources of Data on Nonmetro and Rural Areas

Census of Population and Housing
(Bureau of the Census, every ten years)

Agriculture, Economic, and Government Censuses
(Bureau of the Census, every five years)

Local Area Personal Income
(Bureau of Economic Analysis, annual)

Labor Market Information
(Bureau of Labor Statistics, monthly, quarterly, annual)

County and City Data Book
(Bureau of the Census, periodic)

County Business Patterns
(Bureau of the Census, annual)

Current Population Survey
and other current programs
(Bureau of the Census, monthly and annual)

Administrative and survey data from State and local agencies, such as:
- Employment Security;
- Education; and
- Health and Welfare

Administrative and survey data from other Federal agencies, such as:
- National Agricultural Statistics Service;
- Health Resources and Services Administration;
- Internal Revenue Service; and
- Social Security Administration

The U.S. Constitution called for the Federal government to count the population every ten years beginning in 1790. The primary reason for conducting such a census was to *apportion* (or divide) the number of members of the House of Representatives among the states according to their population. The second reason was to assess the nation's military and industrial strength by counting the number of males old enough to fight in the militia and work in the labor force (44).

According to the Census Act of 1790, the purpose of the census was to learn the number of inhabitants in various geographic groupings, "omitting Indians not taxed, and distinguishing free persons . . . from all others; the sex and color of free persons; and the number of free males 16 years of age and older."

Since 1940, the decennial census has also included the census of housing, which counts and collects descriptive information about the nation's occupied housing units.

In April 1990, the Bureau of the Census will conduct the 21st decennial census. As in past censuses, the Bureau will try to survey every household in the United States. Roughly five out of every six households will receive a short form questionnaire containing the so-called "100 percent" items, or core population and housing questions.

The remaining households, numbering roughly 17.7 million, will receive the long form which contains more detailed questions in addition to the same "100 percent" items as the short form as well as additional, more detailed questions. Households in rural areas will be over-sampled, that is, proportionately more (1-in-2 instead of the average 1-in-6) will receive the long form so that small-area data can be estimated with an acceptable margin of error. Alaska Native villages and American Indian reservations will also be sampled at the higher rate to insure a sufficient number of observations.

By law, the Census Bureau must deliver final population counts to the President by December 31, 1990. These counts will be used in reapportioning representation in the U.S. Congress. By April 1, 1991, the Bureau will deliver census figures accurate to the block level for purposes of state congressional redistricting. Other tabulations and publications will be completed by the end of 1993 (24). (See Appendix A for a detailed list of Census reports that contain data for rural areas.)

The 1990 short form will contain questions about:

POPULATION	HOUSING
Name	Number of units in structure
Household relationship	Number of rooms in unit
Sex	Tenure (owned or rented)
Age	Value of home or monthly rent
Marital status	Congregate housing (meals
Race	included in rent)
Hispanic origin	Vacancy characteristics

The 1990 long form will contain questions about:

POPULATION

Social characteristics:	*Economic characteristics:*
Education—enrollment and attainment	Employment and unemployment
Place of birth, citizenship, and year of entry	Occupation, industry, and class of worker
Ancestry	Place of work and commuting to work
Language spoken at home	Work experience and income in 1989
Migration	
Disability	
Fertility	
Veteran status	

HOUSING
Year moved into residence
Number of bedrooms
Plumbing
Kitchen facilities
Telephone
Autos, light trucks, and vans
Heating fuel, water source, and
method of sewage disposal
Year structure built
Condominium status
Farm residence
Shelter costs, including utilities

Figure 6 illustrates a sample page from the 1980 Census of Population and Housing report, *General Social and Economic Characteristics*, for Whitman County, Washington.

Figure 6   Sample Page From the 1980 Census of Population *General Social and Economic Characteristics* (PC80-1-C49).

Table 184. **Labor Force Characteristics by Race and Spanish Origin for Counties: 1980**—Con.

[Data are estimates based on a sample; see Introduction. For meaning of symbols, see Introduction. For definitions of terms, see appendixes A and B]

Counties [400 or More of the Specified Racial or Spanish Origin Group]	Whitman				Yakima				
	Race				Race				
	White	Black	Asian and Pacific Islander	Spanish origin[1]	White	Black	American Indian, Eskimo, and Aleut	Asian and Pacific Islander	Spanish origin[1]
LABOR FORCE STATUS									
Persons 16 years and over	31 557	531	1 036	419	108 423	1 234	4 341	1 071	14 899
Labor force	16 637	256	530	169	65 792	630	2 309	640	10 227
Percent of persons 16 years and over	52.7	48.2	51.2	40.3	60.7	51.1	53.2	59.8	68.6
Civilian labor force	16 621	256	530	169	65 622	614	2 309	638	10 222
Employed	15 970	239	490	136	60 308	521	1 845	582	8 856
Unemployed	651	17	40	33	5 314	93	464	56	1 366
Percent of civilian labor force	3.9	6.6	7.5	19.5	8.1	15.1	20.1	8.8	13.4
Not in labor force	14 920	275	506	250	42 631	604	2 032	431	4 672
Inmate of institution	267	2	7	–	1 302	28	83	1	114
Female, 16 years and over	15 238	236	425	153	56 398	531	2 435	561	6 600
Labor force	6 967	131	220	41	27 387	222	1 096	279	3 550
Percent of female, 16 years and over	45.7	55.5	51.8	26.8	48.6	41.8	45.0	49.7	53.8
Civilian labor force	6 965	131	220	41	27 375	222	1 096	277	3 550
Employed	6 660	120	204	30	24 630	202	874	245	2 967
Unemployed	305	11	16	11	2 745	20	222	32	583
Percent of civilian labor force	4.4	8.4	7.3	26.8	10.0	9.0	20.3	11.6	16.4
Not in labor force	8 271	105	205	112	29 011	309	1 339	282	3 050
Inmate of institution	159	–	7	–	853	–	47	–	18
Persons 16 to 19 years	5 259	141	141	128	10 299	188	713	95	2 553
Employed	1 496	44	29	13	4 702	25	146	45	1 071
Unemployed	151	6	6	–	685	20	50	–	262
Not in labor force	3 612	91	106	115	4 901	143	517	50	1 220
Female, 16 years and over	15 238	236	425	153	56 398	531	2 435	561	6 600
With own children under 6 years	1 636	27	71	17	8 792	71	472	120	2 430
In labor force	776	7	46	6	4 020	48	241	53	1 293
With own children 6 to 17 years only	1 885	31	39	8	10 617	106	566	122	1 415
In labor force	303	31	25		967	78			903

How to read data in a Census Bureau report . . .

Figure 6 illustrates part of a typical table produced by the Census Bureau. In the Washington State volume of *General Social and Economic Characteristics*, Table 184 covers eleven pages and includes data for each of 39 counties in the state. The purpose of Table 184 is to report data on the labor force characteristics of people in different racial groups and those who are of Spanish origin. These county-level data are only provided for groups of at least 400 people.

The first line of data, "Persons 16 years and over," includes *all* people who are at least 16 years of age in each racial and Spanish origin group of 400 persons or more. In Whitman County, for example, there are at least 400 white and 400 black persons 16 years and over, but fewer than 400 American Indians, Eskimos, and Aleuts. Note also that there is no total column—we cannot learn the total number of persons 16 years of age and older from Table 184. (By checking the Table Finding Guide at the beginning of the volume, however, we learn that data on the *total* labor force is reported in Table 176.)

The tenth line in Table 184 covers females who are at least 16 years and older. Researchers who want to know the labor force characteristics of *males* 16 years and over by race and Spanish origin need to subtract line 10 (females) from line 1 (all).

Row labels are indented to indicate either a subgroup or a percentage. For example, line 1 includes all people 16 years and over, line 2 (indented) includes only people 16 years and over who are *in the labor force*, and line 3 (indented further) shows the *percent* of people 16 years and over who are in the labor force (line 2 divided by line 1). Line 8 includes persons age 16 years and over who are *not in the labor force*. Hence, line 2 plus line 8 equals line 1.

Note that terms, such as "civilian labor force," are defined in Appendixes A and B of this Census report. Check the definitions before using the data to describe the characteristics of your community.

Decision makers at all levels of government, and in businesses and community-based organizations use summary statistics from the decennial census. Here are some examples:

• Federal administrators use social and economic census data about communities to allocate billions of dollars worth of government programs, including Community Development Block Grants, agricultural research, cooperative extension, and Headstart.

• State transportation officials use census data about commuting patterns to plan for new highways.

• Social service agencies use census data to identify areas with high concentrations of elderly people, single parent households, and other groups that may need particular assistance.

• Economic development organizations use census data about education, housing, and community infrastructure to compare conditions in local communities and identify opportunities for development.

The Census Bureau makes a special effort to help the public use their products. Customer Service staff people in the Data User Services Division (DUSD) willingly answer questions and make referrals to specialists. DUSD also sells printed reports and raw data files from the Bureau's censuses and surveys. Call them at (301) 763-4100.

Current Population Reports and Surveys

The Census Bureau also collects demographic information in between the decennial censuses (so-called "intercensal" information). Under a contract with the Bureau of Labor Statistics, the agency conducts the Current Population Survey (CPS) for which they interview a sample of 60,000 households every month. CPS data are the basis for regional estimates of employment, unemployment, income, education, and many other population characteristics.

Because the CPS data are from a relatively small sample, they are not available below the regional level (except for some of the larger states). However, they are useful for tracking national and regional (South and Nonsouth) trends between the decennial censuses. Some reports, for example "Poverty in the United States: 1986," also make metro/nonmetro breaks in the data at the regional level and therefore give us a bird's-eye view of conditions within the nonmetro population (39).

For more up-to-date information about population change and per capita money income in counties and sub-county areas, the Census Bureau

The symbol "(D)" is the Census Bureau's guarantee of confidentiality . . .

By law, the Census Bureau must keep individual responses to its questionnaires confidential. No other agency, including the Internal Revenue Service and the Immigration and Naturalization Service, has access to census records. And when the data are released to the public, they are combined in such a way that we cannot recognize any individual family or person. The same guarantee of confidentiality applies to businesses. No data are released that might permit someone to identify the operations of an individual business. The symbol "(D)" in a Census report means that data have been "suppressed", that is, they have not been printed in order to avoid disclosing information about an individual response.

Business data that are presented by an industry group are frequently suppressed for rural areas and nonmetro counties. This is because the number of businesses in each industry group is so low that particular operations would be easy to spot.

cooperates with state agencies under the Federal-State Cooperative Program for Population Estimates. In addition, many states make their own estimates about more detailed characteristics of local populations, such as age, race, and ethnicity. These annual statistics enable community researchers to answer questions about how the size and composition of the local population is changing.

Other Censuses

In addition to the decennial Census of Population and Housing, the Census Bureau conducts national agriculture, economic, and government censuses twice each decade in the years ending in "2" and "7." Most of these censuses yield data for counties, and in some cases, for sub-county areas.

Reports from the 1987 censuses are being released as this manual goes to press. Those in the 1987 series that have the title "Geographic Area Series" typically contain the most small area data. (See Appendix B.)

Unlike the population census, which uses the household as its unit of observation, the agriculture and economic censuses survey *establishments*. The Bureau defines an establishment as a "business or industrial unit at a single physical location that produces or distributes goods or performs services" (54). Establishment lists are compiled from a variety of administrative sources and are updated continually.

For its Census of Agriculture, the Census Bureau attempts to survey the operator of every establishment in the country which had (or potentially had) at least $1,000 of agricultural product sales in the preceding year. The agricultural census yields county (as well as state and national) level data on number and type of farms, land in farms, operator characteristics, value of agricultural sales, selected operating expenses, etc. The *1987 Census of Agriculture*, published on a state-by-state basis, was released in 1989.

For its economic censuses, the Census Bureau organizes establishment data by geographic area

The Standard Industrial Classification, or SIC, system is a standard scheme for grouping establishments by the type of economic activity in which they are primarily engaged.

Researchers in and out of government use this system because it is so comprehensive—virtually all establishments can be classified.

The SIC system is hierarchical, which means it goes from very general to very specific. Its broadest level has ten divisions (agriculture, forestry and fishing; mining; construction; manufacturing; transportation, communications, electric, gas, and sanitary services; wholesale trade; retail trade; finance, insurance, and real estate; services; and public administration).

Each division is subdivided into "2-digit" major groups, "3-digit" industry groups, and "4-digit" industries. For example, Services (SIC 70-89) is one of the ten divisions. It is further broken down as follows:

SIC Level	Example
Major industry group 72	Personal Services
Industry group 721	Laundry, cleaning, garments
Industry 7211	Power laundries, family and commercial

Another major industry group in the Services Division is Social Services, SIC 83. Advocacy groups, community development organizations, and regional planning agencies are grouped in "Social Services, Not Elsewhere Classified," SIC 8399.

The Census Bureau and other agencies report data about establishments at the most detailed SIC level possible without disclosing confidential information.

The most recent edition of the *Standard Industrial Classification Manual* was published in 1987. It is available in many public libraries and is for sale by the National Technical Information Service.

and type of economic activity or standard industrial classification (SIC), a system which has been defined and recently revised by the Office of Management and Budget. Since the Census Bureau cannot disclose information about individual establishments, fewer statistics are available for small areas. (Appendix B shows the types of economic data that are available at the county level.)

Economists use data from the economic censuses and other sources to estimate the gross national product (GNP), productivity, and other measures of economic activity. Community researchers can use related data to find out, for example, how various industries contribute to the local economy in terms of payroll, the purchase of supplies and other inputs, and the value of shipments to buyers outside the area.

The Census of Governments is conducted every five years and is supplemented by annual and quarterly surveys. Unlike the economic censuses, the government censuses are not covered by the disclosure limitation that suppresses information about individual observations. Thus, the level of detail in the government census reports is greater.

Data on revenue sources, expenditures, tax bases, and employment are available for roughly 82,000 units of local government including counties, municipalities, townships, school districts, and special districts. Private firms that sell products or services to local governments use these data to identify marketing opportunities. Community researchers can use them to understand how their local government is structured and how various government units generate revenue and spend money.

Other Surveys from the Census Bureau

The Census Bureau's economic activities also include several surveys; for example, the Annual Survey of Manufacturers and the Survey of Minority-Owned Business Enterprises. In general, these surveys yield little or no small-area data. The exception is *County Business Patterns* (*CBP*), which is issued annually and is based on data from establishment surveys and administrative records. *CBP* presents national-, state-, and county-level business data by two-, three- and four-digit SIC codes. It includes data on industries which are not covered by the economic censuses, for example, finance, insurance, and real estate. *CBP* can be used to answer questions about the number of employees and firms in particular industries. Because it is published annually, researchers can keep track of year-to-year changes in the structure of local economies. Figure 7 illustrates a sample page from *CBP* for Nicholas County, West Virginia.

Figure 7   Sample Page From the *County Business Patterns* (CBP-86)

Table 2. Counties—Employees, Payroll, and Establishments by Industry: 1986—Con.

[Excludes government employees, railroad employees, self-employed persons, etc. Size class 1 to 4 includes establishments having payroll but no employees during mid-March pay period. (D) denotes figures withheld to avoid disclosing data for individual companies. For meaning of abbreviations and symbols and explanation of terms, see introductory text.]

SIC code	Industry	Number of employees for week including March 12	Payroll ($1,000) First quarter	Payroll ($1,000) Annual	Total number of establishments	Number of establishments by employment-size class 1 to 4	5 to 9	10 to 19	20 to 49	50 to 99	100 to 249	250 to 499	500 to 999	1,000 or more
	MORGAN—Con.													
	Unclassified establishments	(A)	(D)	(D)	18	18	-	-	-	-	-	-	-	-
	NICHOLAS													
	Total	4 905	20 369	78 075	546	327	94	65	47	8	4	1	-	-
	Agricultural services, forestry, and fisheries	(A)	(D)	(D)	4	3	1	-	-	-	-	-	-	-
	Mining	1 185	9 508	29 428	40	12	2	9	11	3	3	-	-	-
12	Bituminous coal and lignite mining	(G)	(D)	(D)	36	10	2	9	10	2	3	-	-	-
1211	Bituminous coal and lignite	968	8 142	23 586	31	9	1	9	7	2	3	-	-	-
1213	Bituminous and lignite mining services	123	863	3 778	5	1	1	-	3	-	-	-	-	-
--	Administrative and auxiliary	(B)	(D)	(D)	3	1	-	-	1	1	-	-	-	-
	Contract construction	187	620	3 176	35	23	5	5	2	-	-	-	-	-
15	General contractors and operative builders	133	505	2 472	22	13	3	5	1	-	-	-	-	-
151	General building contractors	(C)	(D)	(D)	15	7	-	-	1	-	-	-	-	-
	Manufacturing		2 624	11 916	35						2	1	1	-

Figure 8   Sample Page From BEA's *Local Area Personal Income 1981-86*

TEXAS   LOCAL AREA PERSONAL INCOME   65

Table 5.—Personal Income for States and Counties of the Southwest Region, 1981–86—Continued
[Thousands of dollars]

	Burleson, Texas						Burnet, Texas					
	1981	1982	1983	1984	1985	1986	1981	1982	1983	1984	1985	1986
Income by Place of Residence												
Total personal income	127,084	126,771	126,375	136,014	142,934	140,486	197,279	225,046	242,910	282,723	319,090	326,101
Nonfarm personal income	124,320	122,789	121,904	130,352	139,800	137,770	189,053	216,501	236,675	276,423	312,104	319,033
Farm income¹	2,764	3,982	4,471	5,662	3,134	2,716	8,226	8,545	6,235	6,300	5,986	7,068
Population (thousands)²	13.4	14.8	14.8	14.9	14.8	15.0	18.4	19.3	20.5	21.7	22.9	23.9
Per capita personal income (dollars)	9,514	8,583	8,557	9,136	9,627	9,366	10,736	11,671	11,875	13,005	13,954	13,634
Derivation of total personal income:												
Total earnings by place of work	108,724	86,465	73,403	71,752	69,127	61,389	84,355	101,840	108,166	124,635	138,958	144,077
Less: Personal contributions for social insurance³	5,723	4,611	3,931	3,847	4,033	3,632	4,117	5,213	5,667	6,638	7,776	8,047
Plus: Adjustment for residence	−17,277	−2,385	8,320	15,326	19,982	18,409	9,843	7,859	8,178	8,732	10,742	11,061
Equals: Net earnings by place of residence	85,724	79,469	77,792	83,231	85,076	76,166	90,081	104,486	110,677	126,729	141,924	147,091
Plus: Dividends, interest, and rent⁴	19,422	22,085	21,696	25,112	27,884	32,087	60,950	64,803	68,543	85,768	101,117	103,921
Plus: Transfer payments	21,938	25,217	26,887	27,671	29,974	32,233	46,248	55,757	63,690	70,226	76,049	75,089
Earnings by Place of Work												
Earnings by type:												
Wages and salaries	89,212	67,742	54,729	52,371	51,826	44,465	49,965	61,902	66,908	78,135	88,203	90,188
Other labor income	8,708	6,614	5,315	4,987	4,843	4,217	4,946	6,430	7,097	8,021	8,876	9,165
Proprietors' income⁵	10,804	12,109	13,359	14,394	12,458	12,707	29,444	33,508	34,161	38,479	41,879	44,724
Farm	1,597	2,709	3,241			1,485	7,528	7,750		5,545	6,272	
							21,916					

Other Economic Data

The Bureau of Economic Analysis (BEA) is another agency in the U.S. Department of Commerce that makes economic estimates that are useful for describing nonmetropolitan (and other) counties. Unlike the Census Bureau, BEA does not conduct surveys or censuses itself, but uses administrative and survey information collected by others to make its estimates of personal income (by type and industry) and employment.

Each year, BEA publishes a five-volume series called *Local Area Personal Income* (*LAPI*), which contains county-level personal income data. Figure 8 illustrates a sample page from *LAPI* for Burnet County, Texas.

BEA county income data are widely used to analyze the industrial structure of local economies and to evaluate the impact of various public and private programs. Community researchers can use BEA data to find out how total and per capita personal income is changing in their county, and to what extent local residents depend on different sources of income (for example, wages and salaries, retirement payments, and interest and dividend income).

BEA makes its personal income and other data accessible to local users through its Regional Economic Information System (REIS) and the BEA User Groups. REIS includes data files, computer programs, and staff responsible for the regional BEA data bases. REIS responds to specific data requests and also distributes BEA data at no cost to over 200 members of the BEA User Groups around the country. Members of the User Groups (which tend to be located in government agencies and universities) distribute data for free or at minimal cost within their own state. Researchers can locate BEA User Groups in their state by calling REIS (202/523-0966).

BEA also publishes a monthly report called *Survey of Current Business*. The *Survey* includes annual personal income data by county and current business statistics, including consumer and producer price indexes.

For more information on BEA's information services—order the free publication "A User's Guide to BEA Information" from Public Information Office, BEA, U.S. Department of Commerce, Washington, D.C. 20230. Include a self-addressed, stamped envelope (9" x 12") with $.75 postage. BEA also publishes a free list of telephone contacts for data users.

Another important source of economic information about rural communities is the Economic Research Service (ERS) in the U.S. Department of Agriculture. Using data collected by other agencies, ERS carries out research on the production and marketing of major farm commodities; foreign agriculture and trade; economic use, conservation, and development of natural resources; trends in rural population, employment and housing; rural economic adjustment problems; and performance of the U.S. agricultural industry. Although most ERS reports and analyses address regional and national issues, the agency's broad expertise makes it an invaluable and unique resource for those concerned with rural communities.

Reports is a periodic ERS newsletter that lists all current agency research reports and other publications. To be placed on the free mailing list for *Reports*, contact the Information Division, Room 237, 1301 N.Y. Ave. NW, Washington, D.C. 20005-4789 or call (202) 786-1512. The Information Division also issues a free diskette that contains a "Finders' Advisory System." The diskette includes a complete listing of ERS data products, information specialists, and publications. No programming knowledge is required to use the system and free updates are sent on request.

Labor Market Information

Another very important source of information about rural communities is the Bureau of Labor Statistics, which is the principal data-gathering agency on the subject of labor economics. BLS surveys businesses, works with the Census Bureau on the Current Population Survey, and cooperates with state agencies to produce a wealth of labor force statistics. Using BLS annual, quarterly, and monthly data, economists and other analysts can track the level of economic activity in the country as a whole and in specific regions; gauge the health of individual industries; and compare wage rates and earnings among specific demographic groups. Using annual county-level estimates prepared by BLS and individual states, community researchers can learn how many people are working in various industries, how much they earn, and (on a monthly basis) how many people are unemployed.

The Agriculture and Rural Economy Division (ARED) of ERS is the largest Federal unit devoted entirely to research on rural issues. ARED economists, sociologists, demographers, political scientists, and geographers analyze national and regional trends affecting rural communities. Their research is intended to inform policy makers and program managers at all levels of the public and private sector.

According to a recent brochure about ERS, each of ARED's six branches focuses on a unique aspect of rural America (31). For more information, call the Branch Chief whose phone number is in parenthesis below.

• The *Farm Sector Financial Analysis Branch* monitors the financial performance of farms and other components of the American farm sector. (202/786-1800)

• The *Farm and Rural Economy Branch* conducts research on the structure of the farm sector, farm and nonfarm labor markets, and links between farming and other sectors at the community level. (202/786-1527)

• The *Finance and Tax Branch* analyzes the impact of developments in financial markets and changes in Federal tax laws on agriculture and rural economies. (202/786-1719)

• The *Rural Business and Government Branch* studies the organization and performance of the rural economy and its principal industries. (202/786-1542)

• The *Human Resources Branch* researches the geographic distribution, socio-demographic composition, employment, income, and living conditions of people in rural areas. (202/786-1532)

• The *National Economy and Rural History Branch* studies current agricultural and rural issues from the view of the U.S. and world economies and provides a historical perspective on the forces shaping those economies. (202/786-1780)

ARED publishes a magazine called *Rural Development Perspectives*, which presents results and implications of new rural research by ERS staff members and other analysts. A one-year subscription (three issues) costs $9.00 and can be ordered from ERS/USDA, Dept. RDP-10, P.O. Box 1608, Rockville, MD 20850.

Two BLS programs yield small area data —Employment, Wages, and Contributions (ES-202) and Local Area Employment and Unemployment Statistics. For more information on BLS, see *Major Programs, Bureau of Labor Statistics* (59) or call Information Services (202/523-1327). BLS provides a free list of telephone contacts for data users.

Where to Find Data on Rural Communities

Data products issued by the Federal government (including reports, computer-accessible files, microfiche, and maps) are available at various locations in each state. Perhaps the most accessible are the 1,300 public libraries that belong to the Federal depository library program. These libraries receive selected Federal publications that their staff believes will be most useful to local patrons. Appendix D lists one Federal depository library for each state and the District of Columbia.

An additional 120 public libraries are designated as Census depository libraries. Their function is to ensure that Census Bureau publications are widely available to the public and conveniently located around the country.

To find the depository library closest to you, call the library listed in Appendix D for your state or Data User Services Division at the Census Bureau (301/763-4100). See page 15 for tips on what to do if your local library does not have what you need.

Other sources of Federal data products are agencies belonging to the State Data Center (SDC) program, which has offices in all states, the District of Columbia, Puerto Rico and the Virgin Islands. This program typically includes a state executive or planning office as the lead agency, a major state university and/or state library, and a network of affiliates throughout the state. The Census Bureau provides the lead agencies with Census products and training. In return, the SDCs are responsible for disseminating Census products free or at low cost to data users

throughout the state. The services offered by individual SDCs vary considerably according to local leadership and funding. A list of SDC lead agencies is included in Appendix D.

Two government agencies sell data products on a cost recovery basis. These products include hard copy, microfiche, and computer readable reports. The agencies are (1) the Government Printing Office (GPO—Washington, D.C. 20402, 202/783-3238) and its branches around the country and (2) the National Technical Information Service (NTIS—5285 Port Royal Road, Springfield, Virginia 22161, 703/487-4763). GPO generally sells printed reports while NTIS sells electronic data products and typically distributes more technical reports. NTIS is also responsible for making some government data files available to the public. More historic data may also be available from the Center for Electronic Records, National Archives and Records Administration, Washington, D.C. 20408 (202/523-6771).

Useful Reference Materials and Statistical Compendia

The Census Bureau produces four reference publications to inform data users about Bureau activities and reports. The most comprehensive reference publication is the annual *Census Catalog and Guide* which provides a product overview and index, abstracts of all recent products, ordering information and forms, and sources of assistance. The catalog can be purchased for $19 from the Government Printing Office in Washington, D.C. and is also available in many libraries.

The *Monthly Product Announcement* updates references cited in the catalog and is available at no cost from the Bureau's Customer Services Division (301/763-4100).

Census and You (formerly *Data User News*) is a monthly newsletter about new products and issues of interest to data users. For example, the June 1988 issue included articles about 1990 Census plans for counting Asian and Pacific Islander groups; the rate of population increase among blacks; recently published Census reports on federal expenditures by states and communities; a Census slide show on the socioeconomic status of American women; and news from the Small Business Administration. A one-year subscription to *Census and You* can be purchased from the Government Printing Office for $10.

Factfinder for the Nation is an occasional series of pamphlets that describe the range of Census materials available on topics such as population, housing, and foreign trade. Factfinder Number 22, issued in January 1986, for example, described data available for small areas, including counties, cities, and county subdivisions. Several of the most popular issues are reprinted in the *Census Catalog and Guide*. Others are available from Customer Services at the Census Bureau for a nominal charge. (See the *Census Catalog and Guide* for a complete listing.)

The *County and City Data Book* (*CCDB*) is an invaluable published as well as computer readable compendium of socioeconomic data from the most recent censuses of population and housing, government, and agriculture; economic censuses; and other sources. Although it gives little historical data, the *CCDB* is useful because it provides such a wide range of data for small areas. Data are presented for counties, incorporated cities with populations of 25,000 or more, and incorporated places and MCDs with populations of 2,500 or more. The *CCDB* is issued periodically. The most recent editions were published in 1977, 1983, and 1988.

The 1988 *CCDB* presents over 200 data items for counties, including:

- Area and population (1986);

- Population characteristics (1980 and 1984);

- Number and size of households (1985);

- Vital statistics (1984) and health care (1985);

- Nursing homes (1986), social welfare programs (1985), and crime (1985);

- Education levels (1980);

- Money income (1979 and 1985);

- Housing (1980);

- Civilian labor force (1986) and employment by industry (1985);

- Personal income (1984) and farm earnings (1984);

- Agriculture (1982), manufacturing (1982), construction (1986), wholesale trade (1982), retail trade (1982), taxable service industries (1982);

- Banking (1986), federal funds and grants (1986) and local government finances (1982);

- Government employment (1984) and elections (1984).

A sample page from the county table in the *CCDB* is shown in Figure 9.

Roughly two-thirds of these items are also presented for cities with a population of 25,000 or more, and four items are presented for places with 2,500 and over population (1986 population, percent population change 1980-1986, 1985 per capita money income, and percent income change 1970-1985).

The most recent *CCDB* is available on diskettes as well as in published and microfiche format. The printed version is available from the Government Printing Office for $36. See Appendix E for information on ordering and using the diskette version.

Information U.S.A. is a private company that publishes helpful reference materials for researchers. In 1986, the company issued the second edition of *Information U.S.A.*, a catalog of information resources in the Federal government. Although some of the material in the book is out of date, it remains an invaluable guide to agencies and experts. The company's other publications include *The Federal Database Finder* and *State Data and Database Finder*. Check your local library or contact Information, U.S.A., P.O. Box 15700, Chevy Chase, MD 20815.

Congressional Information Service (CIS), another private firm, publishes many useful in-

Figure 9   Sample Page From the *County and City Data Book, 1988*

Table B. Counties — **Area and Population**

MSA/ CMSA/ NECMA code[1]	State and county code	County	Land area,[2] 1980 (Sq. mi.)	Population				Components of change, 1980-1986						Population characteristics		
				1986			1980	Net change		Natural increase		Net migration[4]	1984			
				Total persons	Rank[3]	Per square mile		Number	Percent	Births	Deaths		Percent—			Males per 100 females
													White	Black and other	
			1	2	3	4	5	6	7	8	9	10	11	12	13
...	28 000	MISSISSIPPI	47 233	2 625 000	X	55.6	2 521 000	104 000	4.1	281 000	149 000	-27 000	63.42	36.58	93.7
...	28 001	Adams	456	39 000	1 019	85.5	38 071	900	2.3	4 300	2 600	-900	51.41	48.59	86.7
...	28 003	Alcorn	401	32 600	1 202	81.3	33 036	-400	-1.2	2 800	2 000	-1 200	89.00	11.00	97.1
...	28 005	Amite	732	13 300	2 132	18.2	13 369	-100	-.6	1 300	900	-500	S	S	S
...	28 007	Attala	737	19 600	1 708	26.6	19 865	-300	-1.5	1 800	1 500	-500	S	S	S
...	28 009	Benton	407	8 500	2 541	20.9	8 153	300	4.2	800	400	-	S	S	S
...	28 011	Bolivar	892	44 100	920	49.4	45 965	-1 900	-4.1	6 300	3 100	-5 100	35.35	64.65	86.6
...	28 013	Calhoun ·...............	573	15 400	1 980	26.9	15 664	-300	-1.7	1 400	1 000	-700	S	S	S
...	28 015	Carroll	634	9 700	2 430	15.3	9 776	-100	-1.1	800	500	-300	S	S	S
...	28 017	Chickasaw	503	18 000	1 809	35.8	17 851	100	.6	2 000	1 100	-800	S	S	S
...	28 019	Choctaw	420	8 900	2 489	21.2	8 996	-100	-1.1	900	600	-400	S	S	S
...	28 021	Claiborne	494	12 000	2 240	24.3	12 279	-200	-1.9	1 400	700	-900	S	S	S
...	28 023	Clark~	692	17 000	1 871	24.6		100	.4	1 800	1 200		S	S	S
				21 900	1 500					2 600					

dexes to reports from the Federal government and from states, municipalities, and private companies. The *American Statistics Index* (*ASI*), for example, enables researchers to find statistics produced by Federal agencies. *ASI* classifies statistics by subject, type of data breakdown (e.g., metro/non-metro), and publication title. Many college and university libraries have copies of the *ASI*. For a free catalog of CIS products, write CIS, Inc., 4520 East-West Highway, Bethesda, MD 20814-3389.

Another helpful reference publication is *Federal Statistical Directory: The Guide to Personnel and Data Sources* edited by William Evinger. The most recent edition was published in 1987; it lists key staff people who work with or produce Federal statistics. Check your local library or contact Orxy Press, 2214 North Central at Encanto, Phoenix, AZ 85004-1483.

Summary

Together, the Census Bureau, Bureau of Economic Analysis, Bureau of Labor Statistics, and Economic Research Service provide researchers with a core of information about rural communities. The next three chapters illustrate how researchers can use data from these and other, more specialized sources to understand local population and human resources, economies, and governments.

CHAPTER 3

CHARACTERIZING LOCAL POPULATION AND COMMUNITY RESOURCES

During the 1970s, nonmetro counties grew at a faster rate than metro counties for the first time in many decades. Even remote and relatively small rural communities experienced growth. Economists and other analysts interpreted this "population turnaround" as evidence of a brighter future for rural America.

Now the picture has changed. Population growth has slowed substantially in the 1980s and, in recent years, as many as 500,000 people have migrated out of nonmetro counties *each year*. Of course not all communities experienced losses. Those depending on retirement and government (as in Burnet County, Texas and Whitman County, Washington) have generally fared better than those depending on agriculture, mining, and manufacturing (as in Kossuth County, Iowa, Nicholas County, West Virginia, and Coos County, New Hampshire).

To provide public facilities and services, community leaders need to know the characteristics of the local population, such as how large it is and what its age structure is. To strengthen and diversify their local economy, leaders need to understand their community's resources, such as how educated the population is, how many people are working, and how income is distributed. This chapter explains how researchers can find information like this using data from the Bureau of the Census and other Federal and State sources.

The General Population

Demography—or the science of population—is concerned with the size, geographic distribution, composition, and change of human popula-

tions (27). Demographic change in a community depends on the population's characteristics (for example, the number and age of local residents) as well as on broader social and economic trends in the nation as a whole (such as increased female labor force participation or improved standards of living).

Demographic change affects the local economy by shifting the demand for goods and services. For example, if the number of families with young children increases, the community may need more day care facilities, classroom space, and teachers. Conversely, if the number of elderly people grows, the community may need specialized transportation, more geriatric care, and a new nursing home. People in communities need to understand these changes so they can plan for future development.

The broad question that community researchers need to ask is—what is happening to the size and characteristics of the local population and why is it happening? Some of the specific questions they might ask are:

- What is the age distribution of the local population and how is it changing?

- Are any specific groups of people likely to increase or decrease in number?

- Are people leaving the community in greater numbers than they are coming in?

- Where are they coming from and going to?

In between the decennial censuses, the first place to look for answers to questions like these is the Current Population Reports Series P-26 from the Bureau of the Census. The reports in this series

Table 1 The Census Bureau Works with Individual States to Make Annual Population Estimates for all U.S. Counties

County	April 1980 (census)	July 1981 (est.)	July 1982 (est.)	July 1983 (est.)	July 1984 (est.)	July 1985 (est.)	July 1986 (est.)	July 1987 (est.)
Attala, MS	19,865	19,900	19,600	19,300	19,400	19,500	19,600	18,800
Burnet, TX	17,803	18,400	19,300	20,400	21,700	22,800	23,900	24,600
Coos, NH	35,147	34,600	34,400	33,900	33,900	33,900	34,000	34,400
Kossuth, IA	21,891	21,700	21,400	21,400	21,400	21,000	20,300	19,900
Nicholas, WV	28,126	28,400	28,600	28,200	28,200	28,200	28,400	27,900
Whitman, WA	40,103	40,400	39,600	38,600	40,000	40,100	40,700	41,100

est. = estimate made by the Census Bureau

Sources: U.S. Department of Commerce, Bureau of the Census (45) and (42).

are a product of a cooperative Federal and State program that estimates the population of states, counties, and metropolitan areas annually and the population of places and other governmental units every two years. The reports are published separately for each state, two to three years after the reference period. The estimates are benchmarked on census data (that is, census data are used as reference points) and are developed using administrative records from state health departments, the Internal Revenue Service, and other agencies.[1]

Table 1 uses Series P-26 data to show 1980–1987 population levels for the six sample counties. According to these estimates, the retirement and government counties (Burnet and Whitman) gained population while the persistent poverty, manufacturing, farming, and mining counties (Attala, Coos, Kossuth, and Nicholas) lost population.

How did it happen that two counties gained and four counties lost population between 1980 and 1987? To answer this question we look at two *components of population change*—natural increase and net migration.[2]

Natural increase is the difference between the number of births and deaths that occur in a given area.[3] Fertility, population age structure, and life expectancy all affect the rate of natural increase. All other things being equal, a younger population will experience greater natural increase than an older population.

Table 2 shows the 1980–1985 components of population change for the six sample counties, again using P-26 data. All six sample counties experienced natural increases in population. They did not all gain population, however, because of *net migration*, the second and most variable

Table 2 Both Natural Increase and Net Migration Contribute to Population Change

County	April 1980 (census)	Resident Births	Resident Deaths	Net Natural Change	Net Migration Number	Net Migration Percent	Net Total Change	July 1985 (estimate)
Attala, MS	19,865	1,500	1,300	200	- 500	- 2.7	- 300	19,500
Burnet, TX	17,803	1,500	1,300	200	4,800	26.9	5,000	22,800
Coos, NH	35,147	2,300	2,000	300	- 1,600	- 4.5	- 1,300	33,900
Kossuth, IA	21,891	1,800	1,100	700	- 1,500	- 6.9	- 800	21,000
Nicholas, WV	28,126	2,100	1,300	800	- 700	- 2.7	1,500	28,200
Whitman, WA	40,103	2,600	1,100	1,500	- 1,500	- 3.6	3,000	40,100

Sources: U.S. Department of Commerce, Bureau of the Census (45) and (42).

Census Bureau and other population estimates should be used with care.

In his article "How to Evaluate Population Estimates," William O'Hare of the Population Reference Bureau provides the following rules of thumb about county and subcounty estimates (22):

- Moderately growing populations can be estimated more accurately than rapidly growing or declining populations.

- Averaging several population estimates (from private data companies, for example) is usually more accurate than relying on only one estimate.

- Adjusting estimates to match an independently derived control total reduces error. This means that population estimates for counties within a state, for example, are more reliable if they are forced to sum to an estimate of the state population that has been derived independently.

- It is easier to estimate changes over a short period of time than over a long period of time.

- The populations of smaller places are more likely to be overestimated than the populations of larger areas.

component of population change. Net migration is the difference between the number of people who move into an area and the number who move out. Migration is affected by the economy in the form of employment opportunities—newcomers are attracted by a growing economy that provides more jobs, while people are likely to leave and look for jobs elsewhere when the economy is shrinking.

Starting in 1982, nonmetro counties in the United States began losing population again as people migrated to metro counties. According to data from the Current Population Survey, about one million more people moved out of nonmetro counties between 1982 and 1986 than moved in (8). Consistent with this trend, five of the six sample counties experienced net out-migration between 1980 and 1985 (Table 2). Only in Burnet County (which is attracting thousands of retirees) was the number of people moving in greater than the number moving out.

Natural increase and migration work together to determine net total change. In two counties, Nicholas and Whitman, natural increase was large enough to compensate for net out-migration between 1980 and 1985; therefore population increased. In Attala, Coos, and Kossuth Counties, out-migration exceeded natural increase, resulting in a negative net change. Burnet County experienced natural increase *and* net in-migration

Knowing where people are moving *from* and *to* can help a community or a state prepare for the future.

For example, if people are migrating to retirement communities in the Sun Belt, community leaders might try to offer better services for the elderly. If, on the other hand, people are leaving to find jobs in urban areas, the best strategy might be to give more support to businesses that expand job opportunities for the local labor force in order to discourage workers from going elsewhere.

Using its master file of all income tax returns, the Internal Revenue Service counts the number of in- and out-migrants to and from all U.S. counties (and states) for every two-year period. For each county, the agency calculates how many people moved in (and where they came from) and how many moved out (and where they went). Computer printouts of these data are available for $4.00/county from the Director, Statistics of Income Division, IRS, 1111 Constitution Avenue, N.W., Washington, D.C. 20224, (202) 376-0218.

and therefore its total population increased over 25 percent.

Because age distribution is such an important factor in explaining both population change and the kinds of goods and services that local residents need, most states make county-level age group estimates in between the censuses. A common way of presenting these data is to use an *age pyramid* such as the one in Figure 10. Here, data from the Texas and Washington State Data Centers are used to illustrate the very different age structures in Burnet and Whitman Counties. Burnet, the retirement county, has a large proportion of people aged 60 and older. Whitman, the specialized government county, is home to Washington State University, and therefore has a large proportion of people aged 15–24.

Education

Education is an investment that brings with it potential economic returns both to the individual and to his or her community. Rural communities

are paying particular attention to education in the 1980s as they strive to improve the quality of the local labor force, attract new industries, and diversify their economies.

Education-related questions that people in a community often ask concern attainment, enrollment, finance, and achievement. For example:

- How many adults have completed high school? How many have completed four years of college?

- Is school enrollment changing so that we are likely to need fewer (or more) schools and teachers?

- What percent of the community's school system revenues comes from local sources?

- How well do the test scores of local students measure up to students' scores in other communities?

Attainment data measure years of school completed. For substate regions, they are available *only* from the decennial census and are pro-

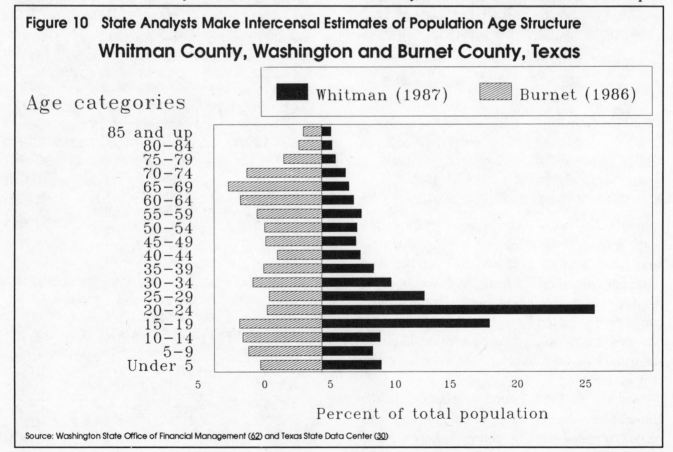

Figure 10   State Analysts Make Intercensal Estimates of Population Age Structure

Whitman County, Washington and Burnet County, Texas

Age categories

Whitman (1987)   Burnet (1986)

Percent of total population

Source: Washington State Office of Financial Management (62) and Texas State Data Center (30)

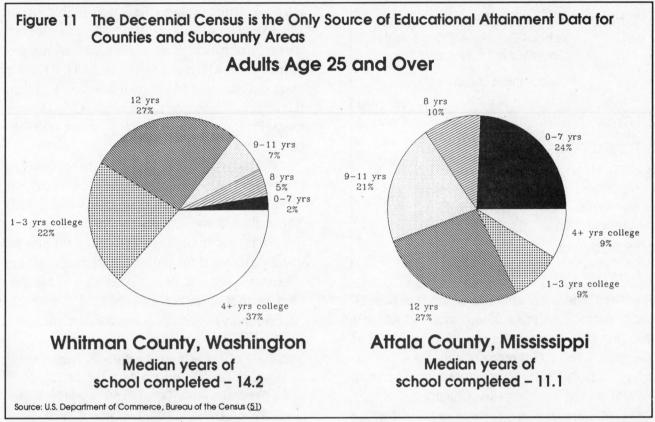

Figure 11   The Decennial Census is the Only Source of Educational Attainment Data for Counties and Subcounty Areas

Adults Age 25 and Over

Whitman County, Washington
Median years of
school completed – 14.2

12 yrs 27%
9–11 yrs 7%
8 yrs 5%
0–7 yrs 2%
1–3 yrs college 22%
4+ yrs college 37%

Attala County, Mississippi
Median years of
school completed – 11.1

8 yrs 10%
0–7 yrs 24%
9–11 yrs 21%
4+ yrs college 9%
1–3 yrs college 9%
12 yrs 27%

Source: U.S. Department of Commerce, Bureau of the Census (51)

vided for persons 18–24 and those 25 years of age and older. The Census Bureau tabulates attainment data by a variety of demographic characteristics (including sex, race, and rural/urban residence status). Figure 11 illustrates how these data can be used.

As we can see, the population of Attala and Whitman Counties differs dramatically in terms of educational attainment. In Attala, the persistent poverty county, almost one fourth of adults aged 25 and over have completed fewer than eight years of school and only nine percent have finished college. In Whitman, the government county whose economy is largely dependent on a state university, only two percent have completed fewer than eight years of school and 37 percent have completed college.

In addition to knowing how well educated its adults are, a community also needs to be aware of conditions in its local school system. For example, they may want to know how many children are currently enrolled in public schools.

The best place to get up-to-date enrollment data for a particular community is the local school system. Researchers who want historical data or who want to compare data from different areas can use the *County and City Data Book* (*CCDB*). Alternatively, they can contact an agency within the U.S. Department of Education called the National Center for Education Statistics (NCES). NCES collects enrollment data from the states and publishes state totals in their annual report, *Digest of Education Statistics*. District-level data are available from NCES on a paid request basis.

Table 3 shows 1980–87 enrollment data from the *CCDB* for the six sample counties. Burnet, which grew the fastest of the sample counties during this period, also reported the only increase in public school enrollment.[4]

Finance is another important education issue. In their study of education in Kentucky, the Mountain Association for Community Economic Development (MACED) found that the quality of education is related to how much local money the community is able to put into its school system. The highest quality educational systems are those in which local funding comprises a high proportion of the school budget (19).

Table 3	The Census Bureau Publishes School Enrollment Data in its *County and City Data Book*		
	Public School Enrollment		
County	1980	1986–87	Percent Change
Kossuth, IA	3,575	2,591	- 28
Attala, MS	4,057	3,410	- 16
Coos, NH	6,849	4,845	- 30
Burnet, TX	3,405	4,469	31
Whitman, WA	5,288	4,646	- 21
Nicholas, WV	6,492	5,640	- 13

Source: U.S. Department of Commerce, Bureau of the Census (41)

The Census Bureau collects some school finance data in the Census of Governments which is conducted in years ending in "2" and "7." The *Compendium of Government Finances*, for example, reports total and per capita expenditures on education and libraries. (See Chapter 5.)

Communities can get more detailed finance data from their state education agency. Specifically, this agency should be able to provide district-level information about how much school funding comes from local, state, and federal sources, and how much money is spent per pupil on materials, administration, and instruction. (NCES publishes similar data at the state level.)

"Making Sense of School Budgets: A Citizen's Guide to Local Public Education Spending"

The primary Federal source of education data is the National Center for Education Statistics (NCES). NCES is housed in the Office of Educational Research and Improvement (OERI) in the Department of Education. Information Services, another division of the OERI, handles all requests for data generated by NCES. If you want information about national trends and the latest education research, call the toll-free Information Services phone number (800/424-1616) to have your name placed on the mailing list for free publications.

is a booklet that explains the data available in most school budget statements. It also identifies ways to locate information those statements may not provide. The booklet is published by the U.S. Department of Education and is available for $1.75 from the Superintendent of Documents, U.S. Government Printing Office (stock number 065-000-00382-1).

The last type of education data that community researchers may be interested in concerns students' achievement or proficiency in various skills. These data come from standardized tests (the Scholastic Aptitude Test, for example) and are usually collected for individual districts by State education agencies. People who want to compare their district to larger areas should consult the NCES report *Digest of Education Statistics*.

NCES conducts a variety of national surveys (both annual and longitudinal) to measure the "health" of the Nation's educational system. Some of their data files allow analyses by metro/nonmetro status. The annual report called *The Condition of Education*, for example, includes selected indicators for schools classified as rural, suburban, and urban. Researchers interested in obtaining data on specific characteristics of schools in rural communities should contact NCES directly.

Labor Force

Economic development in a community is governed partly by the number and characteristics of people who work and the types of jobs they do—whether they are secretaries or doctors, mechanics or librarians. (Development also has much to do with the industries that employ local residents. Industrial structure is discussed in Chapter 4.)

The rate at which people enter the labor force and find productive jobs is an important determinant of a community's economic well-being. Questions that community leaders might ask about the local labor force include:

- How many people are either working or looking for work?

- Are certain groups of people either coming into or leaving the labor force?

- What is the occupational make-up of the local labor force?

The first place to look for detailed local labor force data is the decennial census. The Census Bureau classifies all persons who are at least 16 years old as either in the labor force (that is, in the armed forces, employed in the civilian labor force, unemployed, or actively seeking employment) or out of the labor force. County (and some sub-county) data are reported by sex, race, type of community (rural/urban), and type of residence (farm/nonfarm). Table 4 illustrates how these data are presented for Nicholas and Kossuth Counties. As we can see, for example, the percent of young males who are unemployed is smaller in Kossuth than in Nicholas County.

Table 4   The Decennial Census Provides Demographic Details about the Local Labor Force

| | 1980 | |
Item	Nicholas County	Kossuth County
Persons 16 years and older	20,183	16,176
Armed Forces	16	5
Civilian labor force	9,610	9,553
Percent of persons 16 years and over[a]	48	59
Employed	8,492	8,924
Unemployed	1,118	629
Percent of civilian labor force	12	7
Not in labor force	10,557	6,618
Males 16 to 19 years	1,018	906
Employed	283	400
Unemployed	106	62
Percent of males 16 to 19 years old who are in the labor force and unemployed	27	13
Not in labor force	629	444

[a] Labor force participation rate

Source: U.S. Department of Commerce, Bureau of the Census (51)

Figure 12   The Decennial Census Provides Detailed Information on the Types of Jobs People Have

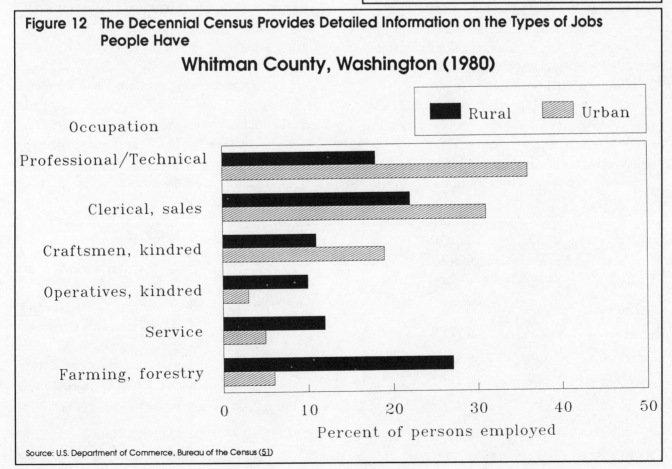

Whitman County, Washington (1980)

Source: U.S. Department of Commerce, Bureau of the Census (51)

The labor force participation rate—that is, the percent of people who are working or looking for work—is one indicator of potential economic growth. A low rate suggests that increased job opportunities could draw more people into the work force, while a higher rate indicates that few additional people may be willing or able to work. In Nicholas County, the labor force participation rate for persons 16 and older is 48 percent. In Kossuth, it is 59 percent.

The decennial census also provides extensive detail on characteristics of employment, including over 30 occupational groups (types of jobs), 40 industry groups (types of employers), and six classifications of weeks worked per year. These data give researchers their most precise picture of where and how much people are working.

Figure 12 shows how we can use occupational data from the decennial census to compare jobs held by rural and urban residents in Whitman County. As we can see, rural people are more likely than urban people to have blue collar occupations such as operatives (machine operators), service jobs, and agricultural and forestry occupations.

More up-to-date data about labor force status are available at the county level from the Bureau of Labor Statistics (BLS), which estimates the size of the total labor force, as well as the number of people employed and unemployed, on a monthly

The decennial census is our _only_ source of county data on employment by occupation.

Many states supplement census occupation statistics with state-level estimates. Contact your state employment security agency for more information. (See Appendix D for phone numbers)

and annual basis. These statistics are issued several months after the reference period on microfiche in the series *Employment and Unemployment in States and Local Areas*. Table 5 illustrates how these data are presented for Kossuth County.

The Federal government allocates funds for its employment and economic development programs on the basis of BLS unemployment estimates like those in Table 5. BLS works with the states to make these estimates. Estimation procedures are explained in each issue of the periodical, *Employment and Earnings*. BLS cautions data users about using its estimates for historical analyses, particularly at the county level or over time periods during which the agency has changed its data collection methods.

In addition to being available on microfiche, recent BLS county-level labor force estimates are also published in the *County and City Data Book* and in reports by State employment security agencies.

Income

Income statistics are widely used measures of economic well-being. Which statistic a researcher uses depends on his or her particular research question. For example, community leaders might want to know:

- How much total income does the commu-

Table 5   BLS Works with the States to Make Labor Force Estimates for Counties

Kossuth County, January – June, 1987

	Persons in labor force	Employed persons	Unemployed persons	Unemployment rate[a]
January	9,100	8,355	745	8.2
February	9,208	8,503	705	7.7
March	9,384	8,771	613	6.5
April	9,639	9,098	541	5.6
May	9,877	9,411	466	4.7
June	10,274	9,741	533	5.2

[a] Percent of persons in the labor force who are unemployed

Source: U.S. Department of Labor, Bureau of Labor Statistics (60)

BLS publishes up-to-date labor force data for the nonmetro and rural population in the quarterly report called *Employment and Earnings*. BLS's annual report, *Geographic Profile of Employment and Unemployment*, contains state-level labor force and demographic data that allow researchers to answer questions about the characteristics of people who are working and of those who are unemployed, and questions about occupations and industries in which the unemployment rate is especially high. Check the depository library nearest you for these publications.

nity receive? What is the average per capita income?

• How evenly is this income distributed among local residents?

• Where does local income come from? Do people earn it, receive it from the government, or does it come in the form of property income (like interest)?

To answer questions like these, community researchers need to understand what income statistics actually measure.

Personal income, a statistic reported by the Bureau of Economic Analysis, is the broadest income concept. BEA defines the total personal income of an area as the income received by, or on behalf of, all the residents of that area, including both earned income (such as wages) and unearned income (such as interest). BEA's total personal income estimates measure how much money local residents have available to spend before taxes (for example, state and Federal income taxes and individual contributions to Social Security).

Total personal income is not a measure that indicates how individuals or families are faring, however. In-so-far as an increase in total personal income can be accounted for by an increase in population, the rise in income is explained by population gain. Thus we use *per capita* personal income (total income divided by population) to indicate the relative level of an area's income, controlled for the population of the area.

The Census Bureau uses a different concept of income, that is, *money income*. Money income is the sum of all cash income, including wages and salaries, net self-employment income, interest, dividends, rent, Social Security payments, public assistance, and other minor types of income. Earnings income is reported before personal income taxes, Social Security, etc.

The Census Bureau reports both *median* and *mean* family income. Median income is the middle level, that is, the money income level at which half of the population have lower incomes and half have higher incomes. Mean income is the average amount of income received by each family (total money income divided by the number of families).[5]

BEA's personal income is more comprehensive than Census Bureau's money income for two reasons. First, personal income is based on administrative government records, while money income is based on income reported by individuals (and households or families) in response to surveys or censuses. Money income, therefore, depends on accurate estimates by the respondents. Second, personal income includes some noncash components, such as the value of fringe benefits received by workers but paid by employers, and return on investment in an owner-occupied home. Because of these differences, personal income estimates for an area are usually higher than money income estimates.

Another widely used income measure is the percent of the population (individuals or families) that have money income below the poverty level—the so-called *poverty rate*. Each year, the U.S. Office of Management and Budget (OMB) establishes a series of poverty income thresholds for different family sizes, ages of household heads, and geographic locations. These poverty income levels come from an index developed in 1964 at the Social Security Administration. The index is based on evidence from USDA's 1955 Survey of Food Consumption that families with three or more people spend roughly one-third of their money income on food. Hence, the poverty level for these families was set at three times the cost of the so-called economy food plan, with modifications for smaller families. Many analysts consider this method of measuring poverty to be outdated (in part because of the assumption about how much money is spent on food), but they have not been able to agree upon a more satisfactory method.

Each year, OMB revises its poverty thresholds to reflect changes in the Consumer Price Index (CPI). Because the poverty level is revised annually, it is the only income measure that reflects the effects of price changes (either inflation or deflation). Hence, researchers can compare the poverty rate from *one time period to the next*. Other income measures may or may not be adjusted to reflect inflation, so researchers always need to find out whether they are expressed in *real* (sometimes called constant) dollars which are adjusted by an index such as the CPI, or in *current*, unadjusted dollars.

Furthermore, researchers should note that income measures are rarely adjusted by an index that reflects price changes in individual regions or subpopulations. The CPI, for example, is derived at the national level.[6]

In summary, there are several commonly used income statistics—total and per capita personal income, mean and median money income, and the poverty rate. The following section illustrates how these statistics are reported.

Bureau of the Census

Based on sample data collected in the decennial census, the Census Bureau estimates three money in-

come measures at the county level—mean income, median income, and percent below poverty. Data are provided for persons, families, and households. These particular county-level statistics are only available every ten years and are not available from any other public source.

As noted above, the Census Bureau collects estimates of money income from survey respondents, who often underestimate dollar amounts. Money income excludes nonmonetary income, such as the value of food stamps, housing subsidies, and employers' pension contributions. It also excludes "one-time" income such as loans and revenues from the sale of property.

Table 6 illustrates how researchers can use Census data to find out how many people have money income below the poverty level and who these people are. In 1979, 31 percent of all persons in Attala County had incomes less than the poverty level (compared to 12 percent nationwide). Poor people in Attala County were disproportionately black. Farm residents were less likely to be poor than other rural residents.

Note that the data in Table 6 refer to 1979, the year before the most recent decennial census. This is because respondents answered the question, "What was your total income from all sources in the last year?"

In between the decennial censuses, the Census Bureau publishes its irregular P-26 series, *Local Population Estimates*. Reports in this series in-

Table 6	The Decennial Census Provides Small Area Data on the Characteristics of Poor People				
	Attala County, Mississippi: 1979				
	Total	*White*	*Black*	*Rural*	*Farm*
Total number of persons	19,646	11,962	7,661	12,439	847
Persons with income below poverty	6,148	1,772	4,353	4,105	144
Poverty rate	31%	15%	57%	33%	17%
Total number of families	3,637	3,320	1,643	5,285	295
Families with income below poverty	680	833	1,027	1,269	46
Poverty rate	19%	25%	63%	24%	16%

Source: U.S. Department of Commerce, Bureau of the Census (51)

In between censuses, we often want to know the poverty rate for areas smaller than those presented in Census Bureau publications.

Researchers use several techniques for estimating these statistics. Some start with decennial census data which they use to determine the social and economic characteristics associated with being poor. Then they make more current, county estimates based on the presence of these particular characteristics in the local population. Others use data from the Current Population Survey to make estimates, either for one specific year at the state-level, or for a several-year average for specific demographic groups in individual states. (See (17), (26), and (23) for examples of these techniques.)

All of these analyses should be regarded with caution. They are *estimates* and are subject to various sources of error. Nevertheless, they are useful as approximate measurements and may be very helpful in guiding program and policy development in the absence of more precise statistics.

clude per capita money income estimates for counties and subcounty areas (incorporated places, townships, and other minor civil divisions). The Census Bureau bases these estimates on a combination of data from the decennial census, IRS income tax returns, and estimates from the Bureau of Economic Analysis. Researchers can use these per capita income estimates to compare their own community to others and to learn about *general trends*. As small-area estimates, however, the statistics should be used very carefully.

Census Bureau reports its larger-area intercensal income estimates in *Consumer Income*, Series P-60. These reports are based on the monthly Current Population Survey. They provide information about people at various income levels, and on the relationship of income to age, sex, race, family size, education, occupation, and other characteristics.

Bureau of Economic Analysis

The Bureau of Economic Analysis also reports income data that are useful for analyzing nonmetro counties. These county-level data are byproducts of BEA's responsibility to monitor and

Consumer Income (Series P-60 from the Census Bureau) is the single best source of intercensal income estimates for individuals, families, and households in the United States.

Based on the monthly Current Population Survey, *Consumer Income* lets us follow trends in the level and distribution of income, and in the characteristics of people at different income levels. All estimates are presented for the nation as a whole, and selected estimates appear for regions and by metro/nonmetro and farm/nonfarm residence.

Researchers interested in poverty, for example, can refer to such reports as *Poverty in the United States* and *Characteristics of the Population Below the Poverty Level*. Some of the questions that can be answered using these up-to-date reports are:

- How does the poverty rate in nonmetro counties compare to that in inner cities?

- Are farm families more or less likely to be poor than nonfarm families?

- What are the demographic characteristics of people who are most likely to be poor? For example, which region (South or Nonsouth) do they live in, how large is their family, and how old are they?

P-60 reports are issued periodically. Some reports come out annually (for example, *Money Income and Poverty Status of Families and Persons in the United States*), while others are less frequent. You can purchase individual reports from Customer Services at the Census Bureau or order a one-year subscription from the Government Printing Office for $47.

measure the performance of the national economy.[7] The agency's county estimates are widely used to evaluate the impact of public programs, allocate Federal funds, project tax revenues, and evaluate markets for new products. Community researchers can use the estimates to measure and track income received by the local population and as a framework for analyzing the local economy.

> ### BEA publishes an annual five-volume series called *Local Area Personal Income (LAPI)*.
>
> *LAPI* contains five years of data on total and per capita personal income, income by type, and earnings by type and major industry. Data are presented for the United States, eight BEA regions, states, and counties. Earnings data are published at the two-digit SIC level for states and the one-digit level for counties. (See page 20 for information about the SIC coding system.)
>
> Also available, but not published for counties, are component estimates of transfer payments, farm income and expenditures, and full- and part-time employment by one-digit SIC. These unpublished county data are available from BEA User Groups in each state and from the REIS at (202) 523-0966.

Each year, and for all counties, BEA estimates total personal income, which is current income received by residents from all sources. The agency measures personal income *before* taxes (like the Census Bureau) but *after* contributions to various retirement programs. Unlike the Census Bureau, BEA includes some noncash income such as food stamps and employer-paid health insurance. The agency reports personal income by source on a "place-of-residence" basis. This means, for example, that income data are reported for people who *live in* Coos County, not for people who *work in* Coos County. (The two groups of people are different if workers commute into or out of the county.)

The major categories of income included in the BEA data are:

- *Earnings* (wage and salary income, proprietors' income from farm and nonfarm sources, and various employer contributions);

- *Personal investment income* (dividends, interest, and rent); and

- *Transfer payments* (retirement-related, unemployment insurance, public assistance, and miscellaneous).

BEA obtains the bulk of its wage and salary data from tax and statistical records supplied by State employment security agencies. Aggregate data on nonfarm proprietors' income are obtained primarily from the Internal Revenue Service. (The IRS does not release individual tax returns.) Farm proprietors' income estimates are based on IRS aggregates, Census of Agriculture county data, and selected annual county data prepared by the state offices affiliated with USDA's National Agricultural Statistics Service.

BEA estimates data on transfer payments, investment income, and proprietors' income on a "place-of-residence" basis. It estimates data on other components of earnings (wages and salaries, other labor income, and employer contributions) on a "place-of-work" basis. To reconcile these differences, the agency makes adjustments that reflect the intercounty commuting patterns reported in each decennial census.

The advantage of BEA data is that they are comprehensive, reported in great detail, and readily accessible, both in published form and through BEA User Groups. The disadvantage is that they are based on administrative and survey data collected by other agencies, and hence reflect an assortment of complex adjustments. Researchers can call REIS staff at (202) 523-0966 for information about how various adjustments are made.

Figure 13 shows how researchers can use BEA personal income data to better understand the relative importance of various income sources. For example, in both Burnet and Kossuth Coun-

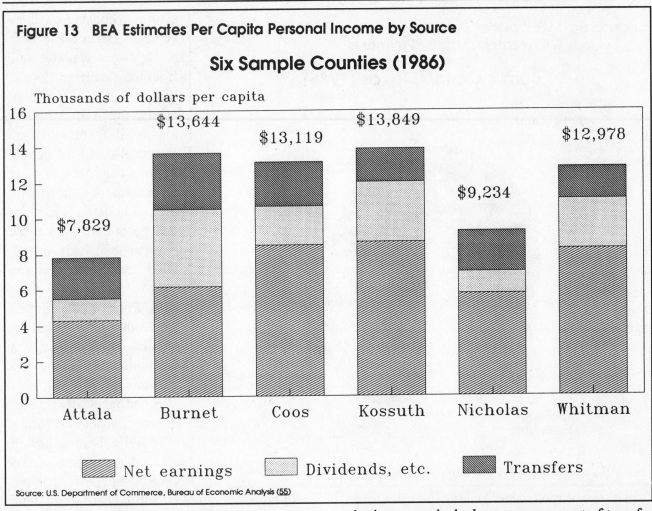

Figure 13 BEA Estimates Per Capita Personal Income by Source

Six Sample Counties (1986)

Thousands of dollars per capita

$7,829 $13,644 $13,119 $13,849 $9,234 $12,978

Attala   Burnet   Coos   Kossuth   Nicholas   Whitman

Net earnings   Dividends, etc.   Transfers

Source: U.S. Department of Commerce, Bureau of Economic Analysis (55)

ties, 1986 per capita personal income was just under $14,000, but the makeup of that income was quite different. In Burnet, the retirement county, unearned income (such as dividends, interest, and government transfer payments) made up more than half of per capita personal income. In Kossuth, the farming county, unearned income was less important, and earnings made up about 62 percent of per capita personal income.

BEA also makes available detailed component estimates of transfer payments on a county basis (through User Groups or by paid data request). Community leaders and development practitioners are becoming more aware of the economic stimulus provided by government transfer payments, including retirement income and welfare benefits. BEA data can help provide a perspective on the relative importance of various types of transfer payments. Figure 14 shows, for example, that government retirement and disabil-

ity insurance is the largest component of transfer payments in Burnet County, accounting for 60 percent of total government transfers. Income maintenance payments (such as public assistance) are a small component, accounting for only about 2 percent.

Social Security Administration

The Social Security Administration (SSA) regularly publishes the number of Old Age, Survivors, and Disability Insurance Program (OASDI) beneficiaries in each state and county, and the aggregate dollar amount of benefits by type. SSA reports these data based on a 10 percent sample every six months, and based on a 100 percent sample every 12 months. Community researchers can use these data if they want more detail on retirement and disability income than BEA provides. (BEA reports the same data in *LAPI*, but in less detail.)

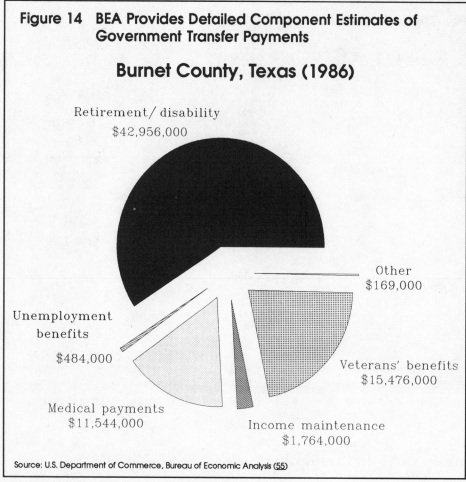

Figure 14   BEA Provides Detailed Component Estimates of Government Transfer Payments

Burnet County, Texas (1986)

Retirement/disability
$42,956,000

Other
$169,000

Unemployment
benefits

$484,000

Veterans' benefits
$15,476,000

Medical payments
$11,544,000

Income maintenance
$1,764,000

Source: U.S. Department of Commerce, Bureau of Economic Analysis (55)

cators of housing quality—such as structural deficiency—are available only from the American Housing Survey (AHS). Unfortunately, the AHS sample is too small to provide geographical detail for particular rural communities.

Evaluating the quality of rural housing is also limited by our inability to define and objectively measure what constitutes "substandard." The Housing Assistance Council notes, for example, that while the number of rural housing units without plumbing facilities and the number that are overcrowded has clearly declined in recent years, the number of mobile homes has increased dramatically. The Council suggests that mobile homes may not be substandard in the traditional sense, but the national standards that regulate their construction do not uniformly guarantee durability or thermal protection. Hence mobile homes are often of lower "quality" than conventional housing (14).

With these shortcomings in mind, researchers can begin to describe the quantity and quality of rural housing. In trying to design effective housing development strategies, community leaders might ask the following questions:

• Do the number and characteristics of local housing units meet the needs of residents?

• Do residents own or rent their homes?

• What is the quality of local housing and how has it changed in recent years?

In general, the data researchers use to answer these questions are available from the decennial

The publication *Social Security Beneficiaries by State and County* is free, and can be obtained by writing to The Division of Statistical Analysis, 205 Annex SSA, 6401 Security Blvd., Woodlawn, MD 21235. Refer questions about methodology to staff at (301) 965-5501.

Housing

Several studies indicate that substandard housing is more common in rural areas than in urban areas.[8] But measuring the quantity and quality of rural housing in small communities is complicated by a lack of data. The Census Bureau, for example, only reports information on housing units that are occupied year-round, and thus neglects migrant farmworker housing. Further, the Census Bureau limits its questions on housing quality to inquiries about the presence of selected facilities and equipment. Broader indi-

The American Housing Survey (AHS) is a good source of larger-area rural housing data.

The AHS is conducted jointly by the Office of Policy Development and Research, U.S. Department of Housing and Urban Development and the Bureau of the Census. An extra sample is taken every four years to provide urban/rural and metro/nonmetro cross-tabulations by geographic region. The AHS is particularly useful in that it provides more data on housing quality than does the decennial census. AHS reports are published biennially on a regional basis in the Census series H-150.

The first place to look for information about the number and characteristics of local housing units is the decennial census. According to the Census Bureau, a housing unit is "a house, apartment, flat, mobile home, a group of rooms, or a single room, occupied or intended for occupancy as separate living quarters; that is, the occupants do not live and eat with any other persons in the building, and there is direct access to the unit from the outside or from a common hall" (49). The Census Bureau will tabulate a complete count of all housing units from its 1990 census and this count will be available down to the block level. All respondents will be asked whether they live in a mobile home or trailer, one-family house, or apartment building.

census. In between censuses, local planning and/or community action agencies can often provide more up-to-date information.[9]

Community researchers can make more current estimates of housing numbers by updating census data with other sources of information.

Figure 15   Some States Estimate Housing Numbers by Using Building Permit Data

Coos County, New Hampshire (1980–86)

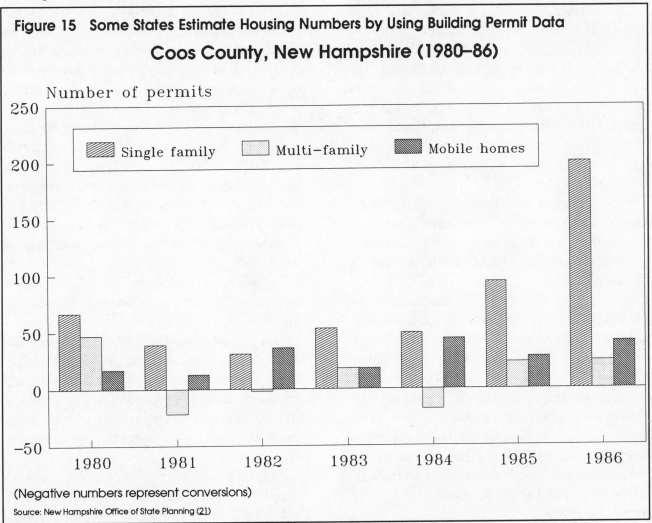

(Negative numbers represent conversions)

Source: New Hampshire Office of State Planning (21)

They can get information on the number of building permits issued from either the *CCDB* or state sources. For example, the New Hampshire Office of State Planning (NHOSP) regularly updates Census figures using residential building permits and annually publishes estimates of the housing numbers in each township (21). Figure 15 shows the NHOSP data for Coos County.

NHOSP estimated that the number of housing units in all three categories—single family, multifamily, and mobile homes—increased between 1980 and 1986. The Census Bureau, on the other hand, estimated that the number of people in Coos County decreased during this period (Table 1). More research might help us decide whether these divergent trends were due to fewer people living in each housing unit, the construction of vacation homes, or some other factor.

After learning about the number and characteristics of local housing units, the next thing community researchers may want to measure is the quality of housing in their community. The size of housing units relative to the number of occupants is one commonly used measure of quality. Small area data on overcrowding (defined as more than one person per room) are available from the decennial census on a complete count basis.

The presence and condition of particular facilities and equipment are also frequently used indicators of housing quality. The most widely used and objective measure is the presence of complete indoor plumbing facilities for exclusive use of the household because lack of plumbing facilities is usually associated with substandard housing.[10] Other facilities and equipment that may indicate housing quality are complete kitchen facilities, telephone, central heat, and public water hook-up. Care should be used in interpreting these indicators however, as none is by itself a complete measure of housing quality. Relevant data are available from the decennial census for small areas (on a sample basis from the 1990 census) and from the American Housing Survey for regions.

Health

The two major health issues facing rural communities are: (1) the health status of the population and (2) access to health resources, that is, to health care providers, facilities, and services. Public concern about these two issues has increased in recent years because researchers are documenting the effects of poverty and environmental pollution on health and because rural health care providers face growing financial problems.

State health departments typically collect health status data. Another, more comprehensive and accessible source of data on rural health status and resources is the Area Resource File (ARF) system, which is maintained by the Health Resources and Services Administration (HRSA) of the U.S. Department of Health and Human Services.[11] The ARF was developed in the early 1970s to help DHHS analyze the distribution and adequacy of health resources in the United States. The system is intended to be up-to-date, accurate, and flexible so that it can be used by the broadest possible range of users, including researchers, policy makers, planners, and program managers.

The ARF is a computerized, county-based system compiled from over 200 sources of health data. It typically includes between 7,000 and 9,000 data elements at any one time. HRSA created the current ARF with secondary data available through August 1985. The agency also has an "update" file with more recent data that have become available since 1985.

What makes the ARF system so valuable is its depth. In addition to data on health resources, vital statistics, Medicare expenditures, and health professions education, the system also includes demographic, economic, and environmental data. Hence, researchers and local decision makers can examine both the health condition of local populations and various factors associated with health status, such as income, climate, population density, and race.

ARF is distributed through the NTIS on IBM-compatible microcomputer diskettes, on tapes, and in hard copy. The diskette version contains about 2,000 pieces of information in four series: the Demographic Series, the Health Facilities Series, the Health Professional Series, and the Update Series. In addition to county identifier codes, the following types of data are available (date of most recent data, including update, is indicated in parenthesis):

Demographic

Environmental characteristics (1976)
Population (1985)
Births and infant deaths by race (1984)
Income (1984)
Education (1980)
Employment statistics (1980)
Housing (1980)

Health Facilities

Population characteristics (1982)
Hospital characteristics including
facilities, bed counts, admissions,
services, etc. (1985)
HMO information (1983)
Nursing home data (1980)

Health Professions

Physicians by specialty (1985)
Dentists (1981)
Nurses by specialty (1980)
Veterinarians (1980)
Other health professions (1980)
Health shortage areas (1981)
Health professions training (1986)

In each series, there is a diskette for all counties within a state. In other words, to get all four series (including the update) for all counties in a given state, the user orders four diskettes from NTIS. Currently, each diskette costs $50. Table 7 illustrates the type of data that are included in the ARF.

Consider the example of a community researcher who wants to know whether predominantly black counties have adequate local health facilities. She could select two variables to study: the number of beds in local hospitals and the racial

Table 7 The County-based Area Resource File from the Department of Health and Human Services Includes Health, Demographic, Economic, and Environmental Data

Item	Attala County Mississippi	Kossuth County Iowa
Population by race (1980)		
White	60.7%	99.5%
Black	39.1%	0.0%
Other	0.2%	0.5%
Number of hospital beds		
1976	82	40
1985	78	40
General practitioners per 1,000 population		
1976	26	36
1985	42	28
Infant mortality rates[a]		
White	7.4	3.4
Black	20.3	—

[a] Infant deaths per 1,000 infant births (1984)

Source: U.S. Department of Health and Human Services, Health Resources and Services Administration (58)

makeup of the population. First, in order to identify predominantly black counties, she uses the Demographic Series which includes 1980 (and earlier) county-level population data by race (from the Bureau of the Census). Next, limiting her review to the counties selected in the first step, she consults the Health Facilities Series, which includes 1983 (and earlier) hospital bed data from the American Hospital Association Annual Survey. (These bed data are presented *by type*, such as obstetrics, acute care, pediatric, and

ARF Profiles are distributed to major state libraries by the U.S. Department of Health and Human Services. They can also be ordered from NTIS. The cost varies by state. For more information on the ARF, contact the Office of Data Analysis and Management, Bureau of Health Professions, Parklawn Building, Room 8-41, 5600 Fishers Lane, Rockville, MD 20857.

burn care, so she can find out whether hospitals in some areas specialize in particular services.) If she wants more recent information, she uses the Update Series which currently includes 1985 hospital bed data.

If the community researcher in our example does not have access to a microcomputer, she can find selected ARF data in paper copy and micro-fiche. These products, which are called "ARF Profiles," tend to be less current than the diskette files, but they are sufficient for basic description and analyses. They are issued as two separate reports for each state and its individual counties: "Selected Geographical Resources," which is a two-page summary for each county of over 150 measures of health resources and "Geographic Trends in Resources," which includes data on physicians; population and vital statistics trends; trends for all health resources; and detailed infor-mation on physicians by specialty.

Notes

1. Estimation methods are discussed on pp. 1–2 of each P-26 report.
2. For an excellent discussion of factors that affect these processes, a graphic presentation of local population change, and a list of population references, see "Popu-lation Change in Local Areas," by Annabel K. Cook (10).
3. In the very few areas where deaths outnumber births, this becomes *natural decrease*.
4. *CCDB* presents these data on the basis of the county in which the district school superintendent's office is located. Because some districts cross county lines, the county affiliation is not always accurate.
5. Household income is sometimes used instead of family income. A "household" consists of all people living in a single dwelling, whereas a "family" consists only of related individuals.
6. BLS actually derives an index of price change for two population groups—one for urban consumers (CPI-U) and one for urban wage earners and clerical workers (CPI-W). The CPI-U is used to adjust income figures. No specific accounting of price change for rural con-sumers is made. For more information, see "Major Programs, Bureau of Labor Statistics" (59).
7. BEA issues its national estimates of personal income first, on a monthly basis, within a few weeks of the end of every month. State-level personal income estimates are issued on a quarterly basis, approximately two months after the end of the previous quarter—at which time the national estimates are already being revised. State-level annual personal income estimates are issued about six months after the end of the calendar year, with estimates for several previous years revised at the same time. Finally, county-level estimates are re-leased about 18 months after the year to which they refer, at which time the estimates for several previous years are also revised.
8. *Rural America in Passage: Statistics for Policy* (20) and "Taking Stock: Rural People and Poverty from 1970 to 1983," (14). In their recent report "Rural and Urban Housing, 1930–80," Kampe and Roman report that the gap between rural and urban housing has narrowed significantly in recent years (16).
9. For more information, see "Housing Data Resources: Indicators and Sources of Data for Analyzing Housing and Neighborhood Conditions" (48).
10. Complete plumbing facilities include hot and cold piped water, a flush toilet, and a bathtub or shower.
11. This discussion is based on "The Area Resource File—A Brief Look" (28), "The Area Resource File (ARF) System" (57); and on personal communication with HRSA staff.

CHAPTER 4

UNDERSTANDING THE ECONOMIES OF RURAL COMMUNITIES

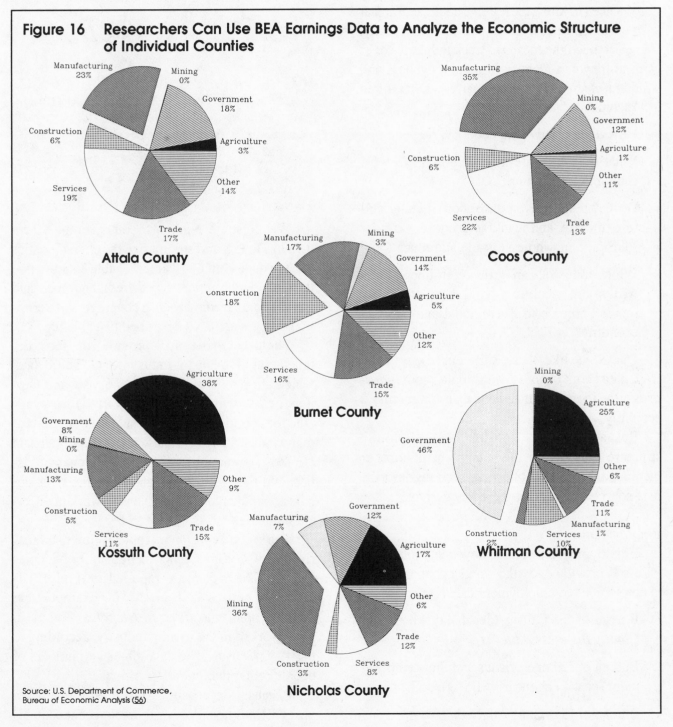

Figure 16   Researchers Can Use BEA Earnings Data to Analyze the Economic Structure of Individual Counties

Attala County
- Manufacturing 23%
- Mining 0%
- Government 18%
- Agriculture 3%
- Other 14%
- Trade 17%
- Services 19%
- Construction 6%

Coos County
- Manufacturing 35%
- Mining 0%
- Government 12%
- Agriculture 1%
- Other 11%
- Trade 13%
- Services 22%
- Construction 6%

Burnet County
- Manufacturing 17%
- Mining 3%
- Government 14%
- Agriculture 5%
- Other 12%
- Trade 15%
- Services 16%
- Construction 18%

Kossuth County
- Agriculture 38%
- Government 8%
- Mining 0%
- Manufacturing 13%
- Construction 5%
- Services 11%
- Trade 15%
- Other 9%

Whitman County
- Mining 0%
- Agriculture 25%
- Other 6%
- Trade 11%
- Manufacturing 1%
- Services 10%
- Construction 2%
- Government 46%

Nicholas County
- Government 12%
- Manufacturing 7%
- Agriculture 17%
- Other 6%
- Trade 12%
- Services 8%
- Construction 3%
- Mining 36%

Source: U.S. Department of Commerce, Bureau of Economic Analysis (56)

45

Overview of Local Economic Structure

Our six sample counties reflect the diverse economic makeup of rural America, as we can see in Figure 16. Effective development work in rural communities like those in the sample counties depends on a thorough understanding of local economic structure. In order to evaluate alternative development strategies, citizens and decision makers need to know the relative contribution that various industries make to the local economy. They also need the means to track industries over time so they can identify important cyclical and structural changes. Questions that researchers often ask include:

• How diversified is our economy?

• What industries are most important to local economic well-being?

• Do these industries produce goods (like agriculture, mining, and manufacturing) or services (like tourism, wholesale trade, and education)?

• Which industries are growing in importance, which are declining, and how do these trends compare to the regional and national economy?

Questions like these shift our focus away from data about *people* towards data about *industries*—the industries that make up a community's economy.

Researchers can analyze local economic structure either from the standpoint of jobs or income, or both. The following sections describe data sources for each of these key variables.

Employment

Employment data tell us how many jobs each industry provides for the local economy. The major sources of employment data are:

• Bureau of the Census (decennial census and *County Business Patterns*);

• Bureau of Labor Statistics and State employment security agencies (SESAs); and

• Bureau of Economic Analysis.

Where to get employment and earnings data for counties —

• Look in the library for Census reports.

• Call the State employment security agency or BLS in Washington, D.C.

• Contact the State Data Center or BEA in Washington, D.C.

See Appendix D for names and phone numbers.

Find out what's happening in your state—BLS "News" reports up-to-date information on employment and earnings at the state and national level. Write Inquiries and Correspondence, BLS, Washington, D.C. 20212 to get on the free mailing list.

We illustrate Nicholas County employment data in Table 8 and summarize the characteristics of each data source in Table 9. Table 8 shows that the four sources report very different numbers and are not comparable because coverage and definitions vary widely, as described in Table 9.

The decennial census provides the most detailed employment-by-industry data. These data, which are published in *General Social and Economic Characteristics* (Series PC-1-C), are available for counties and county subdivisions and for many industrial classifications. Employment data are cross-tabulated by demographic characteristics, and therefore give researchers the most details about the types of people who work in different industries.

The second column in Table 8 shows summarized 1980 census employment data for Nicholas County. These data are reported on a place-of-residence basis, which means, for example, that 2,389 people who *lived in Nicholas County* in 1980 worked in the mining industry, according to the 1980 Census. The data represent numbers of people rather than numbers of jobs.

Because the census is taken only every ten years, it does not allow us to track recent changes

Table 8   Four Data Sources Give Researchers Four Sets of Employment Statistics for Nicholas County, West Virginia[a]

Industry	1980 Census	1986 *County Business Patterns*	1986 Employ- ment Security Agency	1986 BEA
		— number of employed persons or jobs —		
Agriculture, forestry and fisheries	114	NA	27	396
Agricultural services, forestry, and fisheries[b]	NA	(A)	NA	41
Mining	2,389	1,185	1,901	1,948
Construction	562	187	212	372
Manufacturing	1,088	807	977	1,052
Transportation, communi- cation, and public utilities	399	271	275	397
Wholesale trade	213	214	297	333
Retail trade	1,455	1,180	1,423	1,798
Finance, insurance, and real estate	290	228	214	377
Services	1,644	736	774	1,616
Government	338	NA	1,460	1,548
TOTAL	8,492	4,905	7,561	9,878

NA: Not included in this series.
(A): Employment size class "zero to twelve" employees.

[a]Numbers are not directly comparable because coverage and definitions vary widely by source. See text and Table 9 for details.
[b]For BEA, forestry and fisheries only.

Sources: U.S. Department of Commerce, Bureau of the Census (51) and (40); U.S. Department of Commerce, Bureau of Economic Analysis (55); West Virginia Department of Employment Security (64)

For every county, *CBP* tells us how many people work in each industry, what their total payroll is, how many individual establishments make up the industry, and how large these establishments are in terms of employment. Data that would disclose the payroll or precise number of employees for individual employers are not published. (The number of establishments and their distribution by employment-size class are not considered disclosures.) *CBP* does not show separate data for any industry that has fewer than 50 employees, but these data are available by paid request if there is no disclosure problem.

in economic structure. However, the Census Bureau's annual *County Business Patterns* provides more recent (but less detailed) employment-by-industry data for counties. *CBP* reports are issued for each state and include all employment covered by the Federal Insurance Contributions Act (FICA). They do *not* include data for state or local government employees, self-employed persons, farm workers, or domestic service workers. (Because farmers and their employees are not included, *CBP* is less useful for counties where agriculture is important.) The data are obtained from economic censuses, various annual surveys, and administrative records from other agencies.[1]

The third column in Table 8 shows *CBP* employment data for Nicholas County. The data are reported by place-of-work and represent numbers of workers. This means, for example, that 1,185 people who *worked in Nicholas County* in 1986 were employed in the mining industry, according to *CBP*.

In order to administer the insured unemployment program, (Employment, Wages, and Contributions—ES-202), the Bureau of Labor Statistics also tabulates employment-by-industry data. These data pertain to virtually all private and government workers.[2] The data come from quarterly tax bills and statistical requests sent by the SESAs to private businesses and government agencies.

Table 9   Which Data Source is Most Appropriate Depends on the Research Question

Data Source	Basis	Unit of Observation	Where the Data Come From	Coverage	Industry Detail[a]	Geographic Detail	Format	Frequency
Decennial Census (Bureau of the Census)	Place of residence (people)	Census respondent	Sample of the population	All Employees and self-employed	4-digit SIC	To county subdivisions	Published, fiche	Every 10 years; 2-3 years after reference period
County Business Patterns (Bureau of the Census)	Place of work (people)	Establishment (single physical location where business is conducted or industrial operations are performed)	Economic censuses, annual economic surveys, and administrative records	Includes employment covered by FICA (primarily private, nonfarm wage and salary). Excludes self-employed persons, government employees, farm workers, and domestic service workers	4-digit SIC	To counties	Published	Annual, 2-3 years after reference period
Bureau of Labor Statistics and SESAs	Place of work (jobs)	Establishment (economic unit which produces goods or services, generally at a single location)	Quarterly reports filed by employers subject to unemployment insurance laws	Includes workers covered by State unemployment insurance laws and by the Unemployment Insurance for Federal Employees program. Excludes self-employed persons	4-digit SIC	To counties	On request from BLS; on request and also sometimes published by state employment security agencies	Annual; within 1 year of reference period
Bureau of Economic Analysis	Place of work (jobs)	Same as BLS	Quarterly ES-202 reports and administrative records from other agencies and organizations	Includes private and public, full-time and part-time, self employment and wage and salary employment	1-digit SIC	To counties	On request from BEA and User Groups in each state	Annual; within 18 months of reference period

SESA: State Employment Security Agencies

[a]When not suppressed. See page 20 for discussion of SIC codes.

Sources: U.S. Department of Commerce, Bureau of the Census (51) and (40); U.S. Department of Labor, Bureau of Labor Statistics (59); author's personal communication with staff from Bureau of Economic Analysis, Regional Economic Measurement Division and Bureau of Labor Statistics

BLS does not publish the county data but does make them available by paid request. County statistics are also available from the SESAs although these agencies vary considerably in how accessible they make the data. One SESA requires data users to come to the State capital and hand-copy data while others mail computer printouts or published data at no charge. The West Virginia Department of Employment Security, for example, publishes county employment figures annually and mails them at no charge.

The fourth column in Table 8 shows the SESA data for Nicholas County. They are reported by place-of-work and represent numbers of jobs covered by unemployment insurance. This means, for example, that there were 1,901 jobs *in the mining industry* in 1986, according to the West Virginia SESA.

The fourth source of employment data is the Bureau of Economic Analysis. BEA estimates these data annually, but does not publish them because they are produced as a by-product of the personal income estimates. The data are available from BEA itself by paid request and from BEA User Groups in each state. (Call BEA or your State Data Center for a contact in the User Group nearest you.)

The advantage of the BEA series is its broad coverage. Public and private, farm and nonfarm, wage/salary and self-employment are all included. One disadvantage is that some of the data are extrapolated from survey data when administrative data are not available, and so may be somewhat less reliable. Another disadvantage is that the county data are only available for broad industry groups, that is, at the one-digit SIC level.

The fifth column in Table 8 shows BEA employment data for Nicholas County. The data represent numbers of jobs and are reported by place-of-work. This means, for example, that there were 1,948 jobs *in the mining industry* in 1986, according to BEA.

Earnings

Earnings data pertain to the value of wages, salaries, and (in some cases) self-employment

Table 10	State Employment Security Agencies Publish Data on the Earnings of Workers who are Covered by Unemployment Insurance

Nicholas County, West Virginia (1987)

Industry	Total covered wages	Average annual wage of covered employees	Average weekly wage of covered employees
		— *dollars* —	
Mining	64,629,535	33,908	652
Bituminous coal	64,592,967	33,943	652
Manufacturing	15,720,912	13,437	258
Lumber and wood products	4,622,692	13,596	261
Printing and publishing	193,344	7,734	148
Machinery except electrical	1,681,433	21,557	414
Services	8,561,610	11,019	211
Hotels and lodging places	675,820	7,346	141
Business services	1,268,182	16,909	325
Health services	3,640,521	11,306	217

Source: West Virginia Department of Employment Security (64)

income that each industry generates in the local economy. Researchers can get up-to-date county-level earnings data from BLS (through the SESAs) and from BEA.

BLS and its cooperating SESAs collect earnings data directly from employers at the same time they gather their employment information, so the coverage of both public and private sector wage and salary workers is almost complete. Again, BLS only makes these data available at the county-level by paid request and SESAs vary in how accessible they make the data.

Table 10 shows data from the West Virginia State Department of Employment Security for Nicholas County. Note that the data pertain only to earnings by workers covered by unemployment insurance and therefore do not include proprietors' self-employment income. West Virginia issues the data about eight or nine months after the reference year.

The primary reason the SESAs collect employment and earnings data is to administer unemployment insurance programs. However, analysts at all levels of government and in the private sector use the data. The Federal government, for example, uses the data to calculate a geographical index for various public assistance programs, State agencies use them to monitor industry trends, and business and labor organizations use them to negotiate wage agreements.

BEA uses BLS earnings data as the earnings component of its comprehensive personal income series. As noted in Chapter 3 and illustrated in Figure 16, BEA personal income data are widely used as a framework for analyzing the structure of local economies. The data are estimated on a place-of-work basis by type and by industry in the annual report, *Local Area Personal Income*. Farm earnings are reported separately from nonfarm earnings, and earnings from the private sector are reported separately from public sector earnings. The data are available in published and computerized form; revised estimates are available on request from BEA.

Industry-Specific Data[3]

Once people in a community have an overview of local economic structure, they are likely to want more detailed information about the individual industries that are in some way critical to the community's well-being. They may want to look at the industry in the state as a whole or at county-specific data. Questions they might want to answer include:

- What is the structure of our most important industries? Do many individual firms compete with each other or do only a few firms dominate these industries?

- What is the value of production from these industries?

- Are these industries becoming more productive, that is, are they producing the same output with fewer inputs?

For example, staff at the Mountain Association for Community Economic Development

What is the national outlook for industries that are important to your community?

For information about nonfarm industries, see *U.S. Industrial Outlook*, an annual report from the Department of Commerce. (It can be ordered from the Government Printing Office for $24 or found in depository libraries.) For information about agriculture, see the monthly report, *Agricultural Outlook*. (A one-year subscription costs $22 from ERS-NASS). Both publications provide detailed information about specific industries. Authors of individual articles are excellent contacts for more information.

(MACED) in Kentucky focused on the coal mining industry because it has a major impact on the level and distribution of income in that state. They wanted to know how coal production and employment levels were changing, and how changes in productivity (production per worker) affect the outlook for Kentucky's coal industry.

To answer questions like these, researchers can use a combination of data sources, beginning with the employment and earnings sources listed above and with the agricultural and economic censuses conducted in years ending in "2" and "7." These censuses provide data on agriculture, mining, manufacturing, trade, and services for counties and, in some cases, places with 2,500 or more inhabitants. Researchers can then supplement small area data from these sources with information from state and national level industry reports, and with data from other government agencies.

The agricultural and economic censuses are mandated by law.

Firms are required to respond, but are protected by the confidentiality requirement that prevents publication of data that would reveal specific identities and activities. Data are collected on an *establishment* basis. Firms operating more than one establishment are required to file a separate report for each location.

Agriculture

Although many rural communities have diversified their industrial mix in the last several decades, a significant percentage continue to rely heavily on agriculture as a major source of income.[4] The issues facing people in these communities include farm profitability, the environmental consequences of current farming practices, and the structure of the industry itself. Questions that people might ask include:

- What are the major crops produced and livestock raised on farms?

- What is the financial condition of local farmers?

- How big is the average farm?

- How many farms are sole proprietorships (that is, owned by one person), how many are partnerships, and how many are corporations?

- How many farmers are part-time?

Probably because of its historical importance, we have more information about agriculture than about any other industry that contributes to the rural economy. The most comprehensive source is the agricultural census, conducted every five years by the Bureau of the Census.[5]

For the last census, which was done in 1987, the Census Bureau mailed short "screening" questionnaires to a list of 4.2 million individuals, businesses, and organizations that the agency had identified as being associated with agriculture. Respondents were asked questions to determine whether they met USDA's definition of a farm, that is, whether they sold (or had the potential to sell) at least $1,000 worth of agricultural products in 1986. Those that qualified received a complete census questionnaire.

Agricultural census data are available in state-by-state reports in published and computerized formats at the county-level about two or three years after the reference period. (State reports from the 1987 Census were released starting in early 1989.)

More up-to-date information is available from an agency within USDA called the National Agricultural Statistics Service (NASS). Each year, its 44 field offices conduct sample surveys by mail, telephone, personal interviews, and in-the-field observation to collect information on crop and livestock production, marketing, and income. These data are released by state offices in annual reports. Some data are reported for counties, others for crop reporting districts (multicounty units), and still others for the state as a whole. Pertinent national data may also be included in the state reports. Table 11 shows how some of the NASS data are presented for Kossuth County.

NASS operates field offices in each state except Delaware (which shares Maryland's office) and Maine, New Hampshire, Vermont, Connecticut, Massachusetts, and Rhode Island (which are all part of a New England Regional office in Concord, New Hampshire). Questions about the state system should be referred to the Director, State Statistical Division, NASS, USDA South Building, Washington, DC 20250, (202) 447-4020.

The Economic Research Service (ERS) is the USDA agency responsible for analyzing and reporting much of the data collected by NASS, as well as agricultural and rural data from many other agencies and organizations. With some important exceptions, most ERS analysis and research is done at the national and regional level. One exception is the state financial summaries that ERS publishes in the November or December issue of *Economic Indicators of the Farm Sector*, which is

Table 11 State Field Offices of the National Agricultural Statistics Service Publish Annual Production and Marketing Data

Kossuth County, Iowa (1986[a])

Crop	Harvested for grain (acres)	Yield per acre (bushels)	Production (1,000 bu.)	Price received per bushel (dollars)
Corn	237,500	152.6	36,246	2.43
Soybeans	269,000	38.0	10,244	5.50
Oats	5,000	73.4	367	1.83

[a] Preliminary

Source: Iowa Agricultural Statistics (15)

published five times a year. Based on the NASS Farm Costs and Returns Survey, this report regularly includes both income and balance sheet accounts for each state.[6]

Up-to-date estimates of production, stocks, inventories, and other agricultural data are issued by USDA's Agricultural Statistics Board and the State Statistical Offices. Send for a free copy of the "Agricultural Statistics Board Catalog" from ASB Publications, Room 5829 South Building, USDA, Washington, D.C. 20250.

Forestry

The forestry industry includes timber production and harvest, forestry services (such as pest control and reforestation), and the manufacture of wood products.[7] Rural communities that depend on the forestry industry are scattered throughout the Pacific Northwest, the upper Midwest, parts of the Southeast, and the extreme Northeast.

The issues facing the industry and communities that depend on forestry are complex, in part because so much forest land is Federally owned and therefore the focus of intense public scrutiny. Public policy must address questions about how to: insure the long-term productivity of the Nation's timber resources; preserve multiple uses of timber lands while protecting wildlife, soil, and water quality; and afford some measure of economic stability to the communities that depend on forestry. Some of the questions that people in such communities might want to ask include:

- How many local jobs and how much local income depends on forestry?

- Who owns the region's timber lands?

- How are regional timber resources being managed and used, and to whom are they being sold?

- What is the size and structure of the forest products industry?

- How is local employment being affected by increased use of machinery, or alternatively, by the size of the timber harvest?

From the perspective of a community researcher, data to answer questions like these are fragmented and difficult to find. (There is no Census of Forestry, for example.) Forestry is an industry whose level of income and employment is relatively minor in terms of the national economy, but which is extremely important to some regions, especially in rural areas. Therefore, Federal statistics by themselves are insufficient for local analysis and must be supplemented by other data.

Researchers can start with the following sources:

- USDA's Forest Service (which is in charge of all Federally-owned timber land);

- U.S. and state Forest and Range Experiment Stations (which conduct research on a variety of renewable resource issues); and

- State forestry agencies.

Researchers can supplement these sources with information from State employment security agencies, *County Business Patterns*, and the Bureau of Economic Analysis.

One of the first questions that researchers might ask concerns the extent to which their community depends on the forestry industry for income and employment. They can find at least a partial answer in the environmental impact statement (EIS) developed by the Forest Service for every National Forest. The EIS analyzes the direct and so-called *induced* effect of alternative forest management plans on the economy and physical environment of multicounty areas. For example, the EIS for White Mountain National Forest in northern New Hampshire evaluates how different harvest rates will affect income and employment in an area that includes Coos and three adjacent counties (33).[8]

Researchers who are interested in data for a single county, or in information about forestry-dependence in areas where timber land is privately held, need to go directly to secondary sources. With respect to employment data, State employment security agencies collect information on wage and salary workers in the forestry industry including, for example, those who work in forestry services, and lumber and wood products manufacturing. The shortcomings of the SESA data are: (1) self-employed loggers and millowners are not counted, (2) U.S. Forest Service workers are not reported separately from other Federal government workers, and (3) forestry workers employed for wages or salary are usually grouped with those in agriculture and fisheries.

One option is to try to get detailed wage and salary data directly from the SESA and then double-check these data with statistics from *County Business Patterns*. By combining the two sources (as well as data from private companies if possible), the researcher may be able to piece together a realistic employment profile for the forestry industry.

County-level income data for the forestry industry are even more problematic. BEA does not report either forestry proprietors' income or forestry worker income separately. Community researchers should probably work with analysts in their State Forest and Range Experiment Station to develop independent estimates.

Another important question that people in forestry-dependent communities might ask concerns the ownership and management of public and private timberland. National, regional, and local Forest Service offices can provide information about Federal ownership, while State and Private Forestry Offices (located in the regional Forest Service offices), or individual State forestry agencies (where they exist) should be able to provide information about state- and privately-owned forest land.

Federal timber policy is guided by three Congressional Acts that, in theory, provide public-sector forest managers with a framework for long-term planning. These managers are responsible for developing and implementing an official Forest Plan which is revised every 10 to 15 years. These plans are the Federal government's vehicle for communicating with the public. They set forth overall management principles and also specify targets for activities such as timber harvest, road

The U.S. Forest Service publishes "A Guide to Your National Forests," which includes a map of all National Forests, a directory of the nine regional and 123 local Forest Service offices, and a list of the eight Forest and Range Experiment Stations. The agency also publishes "Land Areas of the National Forest System," a reference book that contains state-, county-, and congressional district-level acreage data for National Forests, Wilderness Areas, and other lands in the Forest Service system. Both publications are free from the U.S. Forest Service, P.O. Box 9609, Washington, D.C. 20090 or (202) 447-3957.

construction, campground development, and protection of roadless areas. Forest Plans are available from local Forest Service offices.

The quality of information on the size and structure of the local forest products industry varies widely. Researchers should check with the regional Forest and Range Experiment Station and State forestry agency to find out what is available for their area.

Staff from the Census Bureau's Industry and Business Division handle data-related questions about trade, services, manufacturing, and mineral industries.

See "Telephone Contacts, Bureau of the Census" or call Data User Services (301/763-4100) for names of subject-area specialists. Other good information contacts are the analysts at the Bureau of Industrial Economics (also in the Commerce Department) who monitor specific industries. Call the Bureau Director's Office for information (202/377-1405).

Mining

The mining industry is a diverse sector that includes the extraction of minerals occurring naturally (solids such as coal and ores; liquids such as crude petroleum; and gases such as natural gas). The major factors that affect the industry's performance vary according to the particular substance that is mined, although in general, the industry is characterized by high instability. Analysts have classified some 200 nonmetro counties as "mining-dependent." They are concentrated in the coal-producing areas of Appalachia and the Midwest, the oil-producing areas of Texas, Oklahoma, the Louisiana Gulf Coast, and throughout the Southwest and West as mineral-producing counties.[9]

The primary source of small area data on the mining industry comes from the Census of Mineral Industries, which covers all establishments with one or more paid employees. Information from this census allows us to answer questions about the local structure of the industry (how many establishments and employees), its payroll, value of shipments, and capital expenditures.

The enumeration method for the 1987 Census of Mineral Industries combined a mail questionnaire (for about 22,000 medium- and large-size establishments) with administrative record data

The Energy Information Administration (EIA) collects and publishes output, employment, and productivity data on the coal, petroleum, natural gas, and other energy industries.

Researchers can get a free copy of the annual *EIA Publication Directory* and order the free, bimonthly bulletin, "New Releases," by calling (202) 586-8800 or by writing National Energy Information Center, EIA, Room 1F-048 Forrestal Building, Washington, D.C. 20585.

from other federal agencies (for about 11,000 smaller establishments). County data will be published in the Geographic Area Series of regional reports (MIC87-A), which is scheduled to be released in late 1989 and early 1990. Table 12 shows how 1982 census data were published for Nicholas County. (Note that significantly more data are presented at the state level in the same report.)

Table 12 Mining Data Come From the Census of Mineral Industries

Nicholas County, West Virginia (1982)[a]

Industry group[b]	Establishments		All employees		Production, development, and exploration workers		
	Total (number)	With 20 Employees or more (number)	Number (1,000)	Payroll (million $)	Number (1,000)	Hours (millions)	Wages (million $)
Total	60	21	2.3	64.8	1.8	3.3	51.6
Bituminous coal and lignite mining	47	20	2.2	63.6	1.8	3.2	50.7
Oil and gas extraction	12	—	c	d	d	d	d
Crude petroleum and natural gas	7	—	e	0.1	e	e	e

[a]The Census Bureau used administrative record data in conjunction with industry averages to estimate 10-19 percent of figures shown for this county.

[b]Industry groups with value of shipments greater than $5 million.

[c]Less than 100 employees.

[d]Withheld to avoid disclosing data for individual companies.

[e]Less than half the unit shown. In the fourth column, for example, "e" means less than one-half of 1,000

Source: U.S. Department of Commerce, Bureau of the Census (52)

Other small area mining data are available from state agencies in those states where mining is an important activity. For example, the West Virginia Department of Mines issues an *Annual Report and Directory of Mines* which contains time series data on underground and surface mine coal production by county.

Manufacturing

In recent years, the share of wage and salary workers employed in manufacturing has grown faster in rural than in urban areas, although it has been declining at the national level. In 1984, 22 percent of all workers in nonmetro counties were employed in manufacturing, compared to 19 percent in metro counties. Counties where manufacturing makes a major contribution to personal income are concentrated in the Southeast, North Central and Northeast regions, with a few scattered in the Pacific and Inland Northwest (3).

One of the major issues facing manufacturing-dependent rural communities is foreign competition. Assembly line, "routine" manufacturers (like those in textiles and automobiles) are especially vulnerable to competition from countries where labor is relatively cheap (4). For rural communities that are economically dependent on routine manufacturing, this competition has resulted in plant closings, worker lay-offs, and serious, long-term economic problems.

One source of county-level data on the manufacturing industry is the census of manufactures, which covers all establishments "engaged in the mechanical or chemical transformation of materials or substances into new products" (47). Data from this census allows researchers to answer questions about the local structure of the industry, its payroll, cost of materials, the value of its shipments out of the community, and new capital expenditures. County-level information is presented for the manufacturing industry as a whole, as well as for detailed manufacturing industries that have at least 450 employees in a particular county.

Like the census of mining, the enumeration method used for the 1987 census of manufactures combined a mail questionnaire (to about 200,000 mid-size and large establishments) with administrative records (for about 150,000 single-establishment firms). Data for counties and selected places will be published in the Geographic Area Series (MC87-A) beginning in early 1990.

For larger-area statistics on the manufacturing industry, researchers can use state tables in the Geographic Area Series, or for detailed statistics on specific industries, they can consult the Industry Series (MC82-I). In the case of Coos County where wood products are manufactured, for example, researchers would likely be interested in reports such as "Logging Camps, Sawmills, and Planing Mills" (Report 24A).

Because of the "450 employee" limit, the census of manufactures does not often provide data for detailed industry groups in nonmetro counties. For Nicholas County, for example, the census provides data about establishments that manufacture "lumber and wood products," but not for the subcategories "logging camps and logging contractors" and "sawmills and planing mills." For more detail about manufacturing in Coos County, researchers can use data from *County Business Patterns*, (*CBP*) which are illustrated in Table 13. Among other things, *CBP* data indicate that "logging camps and logging contractors" make up 76 percent of "lumber and wood products employment," but only 68 percent of the payroll.

Trade

The trade industry includes businesses that sell merchandise either to other businesses (wholesale trade) or to consumers (retail trade). Recent research indicates that some types of trade establishments are more concentrated in rural areas (relative to population) than in urban areas. These include food stores, auto dealers and gas stations, and establishments that sell building materials. Other trade establishments are either equally likely to be in urban areas, or are more concentrated in urban areas.[10]

The primary sources of small area data on the trade industry are the censuses of retail and wholesale trade. Like others in the economic series, the trade censuses allow us to answer questions about

Table 13 *County Business Patterns* **Adds Detail to Economic Censuses Like the Census of Manufacturers**

Coos County, New Hampshire (1986)

Industry	Total number of establishments	Number of employees for week including March 12	Annual payroll (1,000 $)
Lumber and wood products	55	530	8,007
Logging camps and logging contractors	40	401	5,488
Sawmills and planing mills	12	86	1,843
Furniture and fixtures	1	a	b
Household furniture	1	a	b
Paper and allied products	4	c	b
Paper mills, exc. building paper	2	c	b
Miscellaneous converted paper products	2	d	b

ᵃ20-99 employees

ᵇWithheld to avoid disclosing data for individual establishments

ᶜ1,000-2,499 employees

ᵈ250-499 employees

Source: U.S. Department of Commerce, Bureau of the Census (40)

numbers of establishments and employees, payroll, and value of sales. In the case of retail trade, these statistics are provided for 10 types of industries for counties and places that have at least 350 establishments with paid employees. Less detail is available from the census of wholesale trade, which provides statistics for only two kinds of businesses—merchant wholesalers (which own the goods they sell) and "other operating types" (which act as agents and do not actually own what they sell).

The enumeration method for the 1987 trade censuses combined a mail questionnaire (for midsize and larger establishments) with administrative records (for smaller establishments). Data for counties and places with at least 2,500 population are published in the Geographic Area Series (RC87-A and WC87-A) which is being released as this report goes to press.

The census of retail trade reports the number of establishments and total sales for ten kinds of retail businesses, such as food stores, eating

and drinking places, and apparel and accessory stores.

Other small area retail trade data are available from a private source called the *Annual Survey of Buying Power* issued by Sales and Marketing Management. Published annually within 12 months of the reference year, *Survey of Buying Power* includes retail sales estimates by selected SIC groups, including establishments that sell food; eating and drinking places; general merchandise stores; furniture, furnishing, and appliance stores; automotive supply stores; and drug stores. Sales and Marketing Management uses census of retail sales data as benchmarks, and then uses other public and private sources to update the census data.

The Census Bureau issues monthly and annual current trade statistics for the United States and, in some cases, states and regions. See the *Census Catalog and Guide* or call Data User Services at (301) 763-4100 for more information.

Services

The service industry includes establishments that provide services to individuals, businesses, and governments. Examples of service establishments are hotels; personal service businesses such as laundries and barber shops; business service companies that do, for example, advertising and data processing; health, legal and educational services; and private households that employ workers in domestic service.[11]

Many rural communities see the service industry as a possible vehicle for economic development. Some service-based strategies focus on attracting tourists (who patronize, for example, hotels and other lodging places, recreation services, and restaurants) while others concentrate on retirees (who need health care, nursing homes, and other services). Critics of such strategies warn that parts of the service industry are unstable because they are sensitive to changes in consumer income and that jobs generated by the industry are often unskilled, seasonal, and low-wage.

The primary source of small area data about this industry is the census of service industries, which covers most service establishments *except* education; labor, political, and religious organizations; and private households. Data for this census are gathered primarily through a mail questionnaire and from administrative records (for the very smallest establishments).

Statistics from the census of service industries include numbers of establishments and employees, payroll, and receipts. The data are provided by detailed type of business for counties and places with 350 or more service establishments with paid employees. Table 14 shows how the data were presented for Burnet County in 1982. (As in the case of manufacturing statistics, detail for specific industries is available in *CBP*.)

Other data for selected service industries are often available from state commerce or business development agencies. In particular, states that actively promote tourism typically collect information on lodging places, restaurants, and recreation services.

The Role of the Federal Government

Although the Federal government provides a relatively small share of local government revenue (as we will see in Chapter 5), it does make a substantial contribution to local economies by transferring income and making loans directly to individuals and businesses. Researchers can learn the size of that contribution by using the *Consolidated Federal Funds Report* (*CFFR*), an annual Census Bureau publication that contains small area data on Federal government expenditures and obligations.

Statistics in the two-volume *CFFR* are very up-to-date because the publication is issued approximately six months after the fiscal year to which it pertains (October 1 to September 30). Volume 1 covers county areas and includes statistics on grants to local governments, salaries and wages, procurement contracts (defense and other), direct payments to individuals (retirement and disability and other), loans (direct and guaranteed), and some other major programs. Volume 2 covers subcounty areas and includes statistics on grants to local governments, procurement contracts (defense and other), and loans (direct and guaranteed).

Table 14 The Census of Service Industries Provides Data on Industries that are Becoming More Important to Some Rural Communities

Establishments With Payroll in Selected Kind-of-Business Groups

	Hotels, motels and other lodging places		Automotive, repair, services, and garages		Amusement and recreation services		Health services except hospitals		Legal services	
	Number	*($1,000)*	*Number*	*($1,000)*	*Number*	*($1,000)*	*Number*	*($1,000)*	*Number*	*($1,000)*
Burnett County, TX	10	a	5	567	6	a	24	4,715	11	705
Burnet	3	a	3	206	2	a	8	2,581	6	443
Marble Falls	1	a	1	a	1	a	9	1,011	1	a
Balance of county	6	3,666	1	a	3	a	7	1,123	4	a

aWithheld to avoid disclosing data for individual companies

Source: U.S. Department of Commerce, Bureau of the Census (53)

Figure 17   The *Consolidated Federal Funds Report* Enables Researchers to Track the Geograhic Distribution of Federal Money

Government Funds Per Capita (1986)

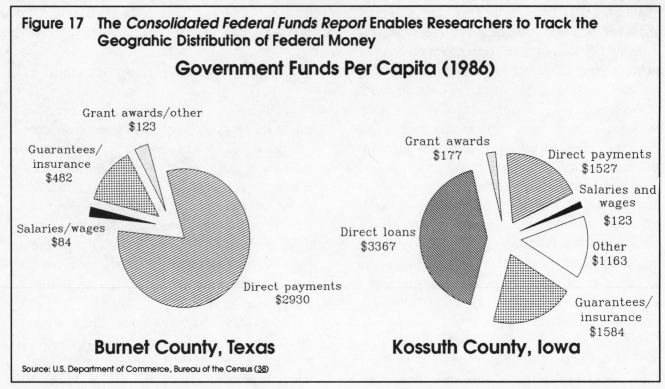

Grant awards/other
$123

Guarantees/
insurance
$482

Salaries/wages
$84

Direct payments
$2930

Grant awards
$177

Direct payments
$1527

Salaries and
wages
$123

Direct loans
$3367

Other
$1163

Guarantees/
insurance
$1584

Burnet County, Texas   **Kossuth County, Iowa**

Source: U.S. Department of Commerce, Bureau of the Census (38)

Figure 17 illustrates *CFFR* data for Burnet and Kossuth Counties. On a per capita basis, Kossuth receives more than twice as much money from the Federal government (including direct payments as well as loans and guarantees) as Burnet. The difference is due primarily to direct loans and guaranteed loans and insurance (most likely to local farmers). Because of its high concentration of retirees, Burnet County receives the most from retirement and disability programs.

Notes

1. Selected *CBP* data are reported in the *County and City Data Book.*

2. BLS estimates that this program covers about 99.6 percent of all wage and salary workers in the United States and 92 percent of all workers in the economy. The missing 8 percent are almost entirely self-employed. To the extent that rural people are more likely to be self-employed than urban people, the coverage in rural areas is lower.

3. For excellent background material on the performance and structure of industries that are important to rural communities, see *Rural Economic Development in the 1980s*, (32).

4. There are 514 counties in the nation where farming contributed at least 20 percent of total labor and proprietor income (LPI) during the period 1980–84. In an additional 540 counties, farming contributed 10–19 percent of LPI. These counties are primarily concentrated in the Plains States and western Corn Belt. See "Farming-Dependent Counties and the Financial Well-Being of Farm Operator Households," by Ahearn, Bentley, and Carlin (1).

5. Between 1969 and 1982, the agricultural census was conducted every four years.

6. Income accounts include net farm income, net cash income, net business income, net cash flow, cash income to farm operator households, and returns to operators from production transactions. Balance sheet accounts include current market value of assets, debts, and net worth.

7. The SIC system used by all Federal agencies includes logging and wood products manufacture (such as furniture, pulp, and paper) in the *manufacturing* industry. Some analysts, like Weber, Castle, and Shriver (63) include these related activities in the *forestry* industry. The latter convention is followed here.

8. The Forest Service uses input-output analysis to describe the structural interdependencies in the regional economies affected by the agency's activities. With their "IMPLAN" model, they predict how various timberland management plans will affect local income and employment in areas that typically contain several counties. Robison and Katzer (25) have developed a technique to localize the IMPLAN model on a sub-county, community level.

9. Bender, *et al.*, pg. 8, (3).

10. See Bluestone and Miller's article, "Employment Growth in Rural Services Depends on Goods-Producing Industries," in *Rural Development Perspectives*, (5). The authors based their conclusion about geographic concentration on a comparison of local and national shares of employment in various service industries.

11. Service *industries* are different from the service-producing *sector*. The latter is a broader classification which includes all industries that produce no tangible product—such as transportation, communications, trade, household services, and government. The service sector is responsible for almost the entire net increase in U.S. employment during the last 15 years.

CHAPTER 5

ANALYZING GOVERNMENT
IN RURAL COMMUNITIES

State and local governments around the country are finding it increasingly difficult to cover the cost of essential public services. In rural areas, declining income from natural resource-based industries and falling property values have eroded local tax bases. At the same time, the demand for education and other services has increased, and some federal assistance programs have been cut. The outlook for future revenue from state and federal programs is dim—States face the same problems as local communities and the Gramm-Rudman-Hollings deficit reduction targets will likely curtail future federal aid to localities.

The message to many communities is clear: Raise tax revenues, cut services, or find a way to provide the same services at lower cost. Making an informed choice between these politically difficult options requires a thorough understanding of local government structure and of how various government units generate revenue and spend money. Some of the specific questions that a community researcher might ask are:

- How many and what kind of government jurisdictions exist in the locality, what services do they provide, and which ones are authorized to levy taxes and spend money?

- What percent of local revenue comes from intergovernmental transfers (Federal and state), and from own sources (for example, property taxes, sales taxes, and user fees)?

- How are these revenues used to provide various services?

- How do expenditures and the level of services supported compare with state, regional, or national norms?

- How many people are employed by the local government and how much do they earn?

The most useful and easy-to-find statistics for answering these kinds of questions are issued by the Bureau of the Census. These statistics come from the agency's census of governments, which is conducted in years ending in "2" and "7." The reports in the government series include data on some 82,000 local units of government below the Federal and state levels, including counties, municipalities, townships, school districts, and special districts.

In addition to reports from the ensus of governments, the Census Bureau publishes reports based on annual and quarterly surveys on such topics as government employment, finance, and public employee retirement systems. Many of these reports include data for small governments in general although data are rarely reported for specific government units. See the current *Census Catalog and Guide* for more information.

A word of caution before we discuss how researchers can use these statistics: Analyzing local government is a complicated task. Frequently, published data cannot be taken at face value because budgeting and accounting practices differ from state to state and from one jurisdiction to another within a state. Therefore, consulting with local planners, people who are responsible for budgeting and accounting within the local jurisdiction, and other knowledgeable people (and possibly hiring a professional researcher) are crucial to conducting careful research on issues pertaining to local government.

Local Government Structure

Researchers can answer questions about the structure of local governments with information from the Census report called *Governmental Organization*, Series GC(1). The most up-to-date edition of this report is based on data from the 1987 Census of Governments and is scheduled to be released in 1989. It provides information on the number and selected characteristics of local government units and public school systems as of the beginning of 1987. County-level data items are: (1) number of local governmental units and (2) type of units (municipal, township, school district, and special district).

Data from the 1982 *Governmental Organization* report are shown in Table 15. We see that Whitman County has 56 separate government units, compared to only nine in Attala County.

For every state, *Governmental Organization* describes each type of government unit and school system in terms of its purpose, authorizing legislation, and funding source. We learn that in the state of Washington, there are 27 separate types of governments. Among these are "special districts" which include such entities as port districts, housing authorities, fire protection districts in unincorporated areas, weed districts, and intercounty rural library districts.

Local Government Finance

After learning about how local government is structured, next a community researcher needs to understand where public revenues come from and how they are spent. As mentioned above, budgeting and accounting practices differ from community to community so it is important to consult with knowledgeable people before tackling this subject.[1]

The Census Bureau reports revenue and expenditure data for counties in the *Compendium of Government Finances*, one of five reports in Series GC(4).[2] (As this manual goes to press, the 1987 edition has not yet been released.) Revenues are classified *by type* (intergovernmental, general from own sources, and utility and liquor store) and expenditures are classified *by function*. (Functions include education services, social service and income maintenance, transportation, public safety, environment and housing, government administration, and utilities.)

Figure 18 illustrates how a researcher might use these revenue data. For all six sample counties, revenue from the

---

Table 15 *Governmental Organization*, a Report from the Census of Governments, is a Primer on Local Governments and Public School Systems

Governmental Units: 1982

County	Total[a]	Municipal	School District	Special District Total	Special District With property taxing power
			— number —		
Attala, Mississippi	9	4	2	2	0
Burnet, Texas	13	4	2	6	0
Coos, New Hampshire	44	1	15	8	2
Kossuth, Iowa	21	12	7	1	0
Nicholas, West Virginia	12	2	1	8	0
Whitman, Washington	56	16	13	26	24

[a]Includes county government as a separate unit. Coos County total includes 19 township units.

Source: U.S. Department of Commerce, Bureau of the Census (46)

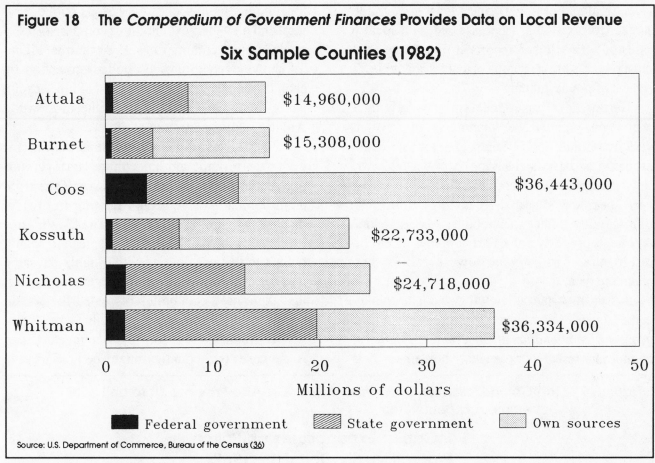

Figure 18   The *Compendium of Government Finances* Provides Data on Local Revenue

Six Sample Counties (1982)

Federal government ▨ State government ☐ Own sources

Source: U.S. Department of Commerce, Bureau of the Census (36)

Federal government to the county (not including money paid directly to individuals) makes up the smallest share of total revenue. Coos County gets the largest share from the Federal government because so much of the county is made up of Forest Service land. Whitman County, on the other hand, generates the largest share from state sources, primarily because of its state university.

Own source revenue, which is money raised by the county itself, comes from two sources. The first is taxes (such as real property, personal property, income and sales). The second source is charges and miscellaneous revenues (such as interest earnings, fees and permit revenue, and user fees for water, solid waste disposal, recreation, etc.)

One very important component of own source revenue is the property tax. When property tax revenues fluctuate from year-to-year (as they do in some resource-based rural communities), providing public services that depend on property taxes is especially difficult. For example, between 1982 and 1986, plummeting land values in many farm-dependent communities caused property tax collections to decline. This placed severe stress on the ability of local governments to finance education and other public services (29).

One source of data for analyzing local property tax values is the Census report called *Taxable Property Values and Assessment/Sales Price Ratios*, Series GC(2). It contains information on assessed valuations, property sales, and property tax rates. County-level data items are: (1) gross assessed property value (total, real, and personal); (2) the tax-exempt portion of locally assessed

> ## Sources of comparative finance data may be available in your state for years in between the censuses.
>
> Contact your county, municipal, or school district officials, state association of counties or municipalities, the state auditor, or private associations such as the state taxpayers' league.

value (real and personal); and (3) assessed value subject to tax (total, state assessed, and locally assessed). Like other reports in this series, the most recent edition is based on data from the 1987 census of governments.

Because local governments must make budget projections annually or biannually, it is often very important for officials to know how the property tax base is changing from year to year. Because Census data are issued only every five years, people who need more up-to-date information should contact their county tax assessor.[3] Although property values are a matter of public record, assessors vary in how accessible they make the data.

Just as important as knowing where the money comes from is knowing how it is spent. Again using the *Compendium of Government Finances*, community researchers can learn how much their local government spends on various public services, and how their expenditures compare to those made in other communities. For example, Figure 19 shows expenditures on police protection by each of the six sample counties. On a per capita basis, Whitman County spends the most while Attala County spends the least.

Other tables in this Census report show (for each state) revenue and expenditure data for groups of counties of similar population size. (There are eight population-size groups ranging from "less than 10,000" to "1,000,000 or more.") With this information, researchers can compare their county budget to that of counties with roughly the same number of people. They might, for example, learn that there are "economies of scale" for certain services, that is, the cost of providing a particular service might be less for larger counties. If this is the case, two counties might be able to save

Figure 19   The *Compendium of Government Finances* Also Provides Data on Local Government Expenditures

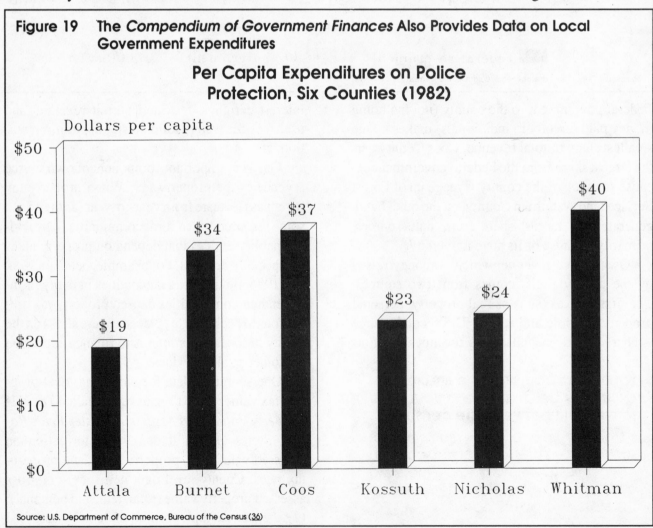

Per Capita Expenditures on Police Protection, Six Counties (1982)

Dollars per capita

Source: U.S. Department of Commerce, Bureau of the Census (36)

money if they offer the service jointly instead of individually. (Alternatively, the cost of providing services might be affected by population density rather than size, a relationship that the Census data would not reveal.)

Public Employment

Public employee payroll is one of the largest components of local government expenditures and is one target for budget cuts in some parts of the Nation. Using Census data, researchers can find out how many people are employed to provide public services in their county. They can also compare their public employment and payroll levels to those in counties of similar size around the country.

The source of such information is a report called *Public Employment*, Series GC(3). One of the volumes in this report, *Compendium of Public Employment*, includes county-level data on number of employees by function as well as October earnings for full-time teachers and all other public employees.

Figure 20 illustrates how these data can be used. Of the six sample counties, local government hired the most full-time equivalent (FTE) teachers per 1,000 population in Nicholas County, and the least in Whitman County. In October 1982, these teachers earned the highest salary in Whitman County and the lowest in Attala County.

Again, Census issues these data only once every five years, so people who need more up-to-date data should contact local sources, such as their county or municipal government office.

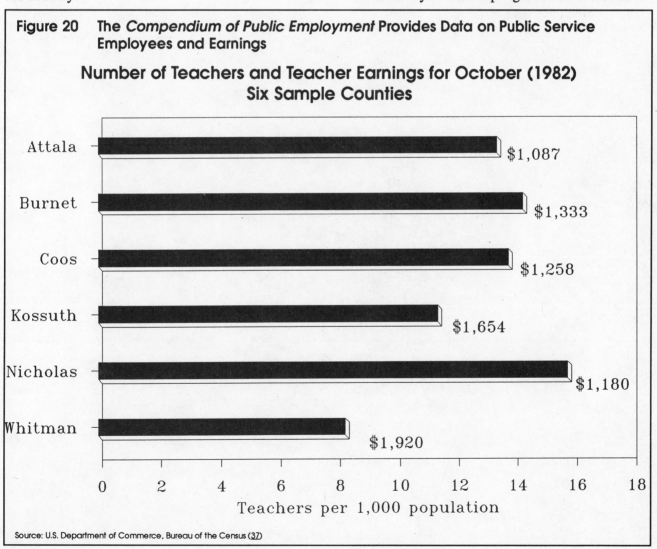

Figure 20   The *Compendium of Public Employment* Provides Data on Public Service Employees and Earnings

Number of Teachers and Teacher Earnings for October (1982) Six Sample Counties

Attala — $1,087

Burnet — $1,333

Coos — $1,258

Kossuth — $1,654

Nicholas — $1,180

Whitman — $1,920

Teachers per 1,000 population

Source: U.S. Department of Commerce, Bureau of the Census (37)

Notes

1. Government accounts are usually organized into distinct funds which are kept separate for the purpose of carrying out specific activities or achieving particular objectives. Three important types of funds are: 1) general government, through which most governmental functions are financed; 2) proprietary, which accounts for private sector-type activities; and 3) fiduciary, which accounts for assets held by the government in an agent or trustee capacity (12). For more information on government accounting procedures, consult a textbook on local government finance.

2. Other reports in the series present larger-area data on government revenues, by source and type; expenditures, by function, character, and object; indebtedness and debt transactions; and cash and security holdings.

3. In some states, funding formulas provide incentives for communities to assess property at less than fair market value. Where these incentives are large, people may get more accurate information about local property values from the State Department of Revenue or State Board of Equalization than from local officials.

REFERENCES

1. Ahearn, Mary, Susan Bentley, and Thomas Carlin. "Farming-Dependent Counties and the Financial Well-Being of Farm Operator Households," United States Department of Agriculture, Economic Research Service, Agriculture Information Bulletin No. 544, August 1988.

2. Babbie, Earl. *The Practice of Social Research*, Fourth Edition, Wadsdworth Publishing Company, Belmont, California, 1986.

3. Bender, *et al*. "The Diverse Social and Economic Structure of Nonmetropolitan America," United States Department of Agriculture, Economic Research Service, Rural Development Research Report Number 49, September 1985.

4. Bloomquist, Leonard. "Rural Manufacturing Gets Mixed Reviews," *Rural Development Perspectives*, Vol. 4, No. 3, June 1988.

5. Bluestone, Herman, and Tom Miller. "Employment Growth in Rural Services Depends on Goods-Producing Industries," *Rural Development Perspectives*, Vol. 4, No. 2, February 1988.

6. Bonnen, James T. "Improving Information on Agriculture and Rural Life," *American Journal of Agricultural Economics*, Vol. 57, No. 5, December 1975.

7. _____. "The Statistical Data Base for Rural America," Staff Paper No. 88-80, Department of Agricultural Economics, Michigan State University, October 1988.

8. Brown, David L. and Kenneth L. Deavers. "Rural Change and the Rural Economic Policy Agenda for the 1980s," in *Rural Economic Development in the 1980s*, pp. 1–23, Economic Research Staff Report AGES870724, July 1987.

9. Community Information Exchange. "Computers for Neighborhoods," second edition, Washington, D.C., 1987.

10. Cook, Annabel K. "Population Change in Local Areas," WREP 93, Western Rural Development Center, Oregon State University, Corvallis (undated).

11. Duncan, Cynthia M. "Gaps in Our Understanding of Rural Communities," remarks prepared as discussant, "Toward Rural Development Policy for the 1990s: Enhancing Income and Employment Opportunities," a symposium sponsored by the Congressional Research Service and Joint Economic Committee of Congress, September 1988.

12. Government Finance Officers Association. *Financial Management Handbook for Local Governments*, Chicago, 1986.

13. Guralink, David, Editor-in-Chief. *New World Dictionary: Second College Edition*, William Collins and World Publishing Co., Inc., 1978.

14. Housing Assistance Council. "Taking Stock: Rural People and Poverty from 1970 to 1983," Washington, D.C., 1984.

15. Iowa Agricultural Statistics. "1987 Agricultural Statistics," Iowa Department of Agriculture and Land Stewardship," Des Moines, June 1987.

16. Kampe, Ronald, and Gail Roman. "Rural and Urban Housing, 1930–80," United States Department of Agriculture, Economic Research Service, ARED Staff Report AGES871210, December 1988.

17. Koebel, C. Theodore, and Michael Price. "Kentucky Poverty Rates," in *Newsletter from the State Data Center of Kentucky*, Vol. 7, No. 1, Louisville, KY, Winter 1989.

18. Manka, Paul T. "A Fiche Story," in *American Demographics*, May 1982.

19. Mountain Association for Community Economic Development. "Would You Like to Swing on a Star? A report to the Shakertown Roundtable Conference on Economic Development and Education in Kentucky's Fifth Congressional District," Berea, Kentucky, May 1986.

20. National Research Council, Panel on Statistics for Rural Development Policy. *Rural America in Passage: Statistics for Policy*, National Academy Press, Washington, D.C., December 1981.

21. New Hampshire Office of State Planning. "Current Estimates and Trends in New Hampshire's Housing Supply, Update: 1986," Concord, New Hampshire, 1987.

22. O'Hare, William. "How to Evaluate Population Estimates," *American Demographics*, January 1988.

23. Plotnick, Robert D. "Rural Poverty in the Northwest: New Findings and Policy Implications," *Northwest Report*, Northwest Area Foundation, No. 7, March 1989.

24. Riley, David. "The Big Count," in *Government Executive*, April 1988.

25. Robison, M. H., and Scott Katzer. "The Impact of a Timber Shortage on the Economy of the West-Central Idaho Highlands," Department of Forest Resources, University of Idaho, unpublished, 1989.

26. Ross, Christine M., and Sheldon Danziger. "Poverty Rates by State, 1979 and 1985: A Research Note," *Focus*, Vol. 10, No. 3, Madison, WI, Fall 1987.

27. Shryock, Henry S., Jacob S. Siegel, and Associates. *The Methods and Materials of Demography*, Fourth Printing (Rev.), United States Department of Commerce, Washington, D.C., June 1980.

28. Stambler, Howard V. "The Area Resource File—A Brief Look," *Public Health Reports*, Vol. 103, No. 2, March–April 1988.

29. Subcommittee on Intergovernmental Relations of the Committee on Governmental Affairs. "Governing the Heartland: Can Rural Governments Survive the Farm Crisis," Committee Print 99–176, United States Government Printing Office, Washington, D.C., 1986.

30. Texas State Data Center. Data request by author, 1988.

31. United States Department of Agriculture, Economic Research Service. "The Economic Research Service in 1989," Washington, D.C., April 1989.

32. _____. *Rural Economic Development in the 1980s*, Economic Research Service Staff Report, AGES870724, July 1987.

33. United States Department of Agriculture, Forest Service, Eastern Region. "Record of Decision, Final Environmental Impact

Statement, Land and Resource Management Plan, White Mountain National Forest," April 1986.

34. United States Department of Commerce, Bureau of the Census. *Census Catalog and Guide: 1987*, June 1987.

35. _____. "Census Geography—Concepts and Products," CFF, No. 8 (Rev.), August 1985.

36. _____. *Compendium of Government Finances*, GC82(4)-5, December 1984.

37. _____. *Compendium of Public Employment*, GC82(3)-2, December 1984.

38. _____. *Consolidated Federal Funds Report: Fiscal Year 1986*, March 1987.

39. _____. *Consumer Income*, Series P-60, No. 160, June 1988.

40. _____. *County Business Patterns*, CBP-86, selected issues, 1988.

41. _____. *County and City Data Book, 1988*, (published and files on diskette), 1988.

42. _____. *County Population Estimates: July 1, 1987 and 1986*, CPR Series P-26, No. 87-A, September 1988.

43. _____. "Data for Small Communities," CFF No. 22 (Rev.), January 1986.

44. _____. "Educator's Guide to the 1990 Census," D-3300C, August 1988.

45. _____. *Estimates of the Population of (State) Counties and Metropolitan Areas: July 1, 1981–July 1, 1985*, CPR Series P-26, No. 85-(state)-C, selected issues.

46. _____. *Governmental Organization*, GS82 (1)-1, 1983.

47. _____. *Guide to the 1987 Economic Censuses and Related Statistics*, forthcoming.

48. _____. "Housing Data Resources: Indicators and Sources of Data for Analyzing Housing and Neighborhood Conditions," United States Government Printing Office, 1980.

49. _____. "Housing Statistics," CFF No. 6 (Rev.), December 1981.

50. _____. "New Standards for Metropolitan Statistical Areas," in *Data User News*, Vol. 15, No. 6, June 1980.

51. _____. *1980 Census of Population, General Social and Economic Characteristics*, PC80-1-C, selected issues, 1983.

52. _____. *1982 Census of Mineral Industries*, MIC82-A-5, 1985.

53. _____. *1982 Census of Service Industries*, SC82-A-44, 1984.

54. _____. "A Preview of the 1987 Economic Censuses," EC-87-1 (Rev.), undated.

55. United States Department of Commerce, Bureau of Economic Analysis, Regional Economic Information System. Data request by author, 1988.

56. _____. *Local Area Personal Income: 1981-1986*, July 1988.

57. United States Department of Health and Human Services, Public Health Service, Health Resources and Services Administration. "The Area Resource File (ARF) System," ODAM Report No. 6-88, June 1988.

58. _____. "County Profiles," selected issues, 1989.

59. United States Department of Labor, Bureau of Labor Statistics. *Major Programs: Bureau of Labor Statistics*, Report 693, June 1983.

60. _____. *Unemployment in States and Local Areas*, January–October 1987, issues on microfiche, November 1987.

61. Wallman, Katherine K. "Losing Count: The Federal Statistical System," Population Trends and Public Policy Paper No. 16, Population Reference Bureau, Washington, D.C., September 1988.

62. Washington State Office of Financial Management. *State of Washington Data Book: 1987*, Olympia, 1988.

63. Weber, Bruce A., Emery N. Castle, and Ann L. Shriver. "The Performance of Natural Resource Industries," *Rural Economic Development for the 1980s*, Economic Research Service Staff Report AGES870724, July 1987.

64. West Virginia Department of Employment Security. *Employment and Wages*, selected issues, LER 201, Charleston.

GLOSSARY*

administrative data

Data collected in the course of an organization's normal business, for example, the Internal Revenue Service's file of all income tax returns.

age pyramid

A bar graph that shows the age distribution of a population. Age pyramids are usually constructed using 5-year intervals, with the older age intervals at the top of the graph.

aggregate income

See *total personal income*.

Beale coding system

Classifies all U.S. counties into ten groups based on urban/rural population characteristics and location with respect to urban areas. Includes six groups of nonmetro counties and four groups of metro counties. Also referred to as the "Urban-Rural Continuum Code."

block

The Census Bureau term for a small geographic area with discernable boundaries but no minimum population. Blocks are the smallest geographic units used by the Census Bureau for collecting and reporting data. In rural areas, block boundaries may be visible features such as roads, powerlines, fences, and abandoned railroads.

census

A count, or enumeration, of the population.

census county division (CCD)

A county subdivision designated by the Census Bureau for statistical purposes in states where *minor civil divisions* do not exist.

census designated place (CDP)

The Census Bureau term for an unincorporated, closely settled population center with at least 1,000 inhabitants and without legally established boundaries. CDPs are designated for statistical purposes.

consumer price index (CPI)

A single number which gives the average value of current consumer prices compared to some base period. Compiled by the Bureau of Labor Statistics, the CPI measures how much inflation (or deflation) is occurring across the entire range of consumer goods.

constant dollars

See *real dollars*.

current dollars

Dollars that have not been adjusted by a price index (such as the *consumer price index*), as contrasted with *real dollars*.

decennial census

A *census* taken every ten years. The U.S. Census Bureau conducts a decennial census of population and housing in years ending in 0 (zero).

---

* For more detail, readers are encouraged to refer to original sources referenced in the text.

demography

A science concerned with the size, geographic distribution, structure, and change of human populations. Demographic statistics include those that pertain to population, sex, and age composition, mortality and fertility, educational and economic characteristics, and migration.

enumeration district

The Census Bureau term for a geographical area assigned to one *enumerator*.

enumeration method

The method by which data are collected, for example, with a mail questionnaire, personal interview, or from administrative records.

enumerator

In the case of the decennial census, an employee of the Census Bureau who is hired to count housing units and personally interview a sample of the population. More generally, a person who conducts interviews.

environmental impact statement (EIS)

In the case of the U.S. Forest Service, an analysis of the direct and indirect effects of alternative forest management plans on the economy and physical environment of a multi-county area. More generally, an analysis of how a particular development project will affect resource use and quality in a particular area.

industry

Kind of establishment; an establishment's economic activity, such as agriculture, medical services, construction, or retail trade.

intercensal

Between the years of the *decennial census*. Working with State agencies, the Census Bureau makes intercensal estimates of the population of all U.S. counties and subcounty governmental units.

labor and proprietor income (LPI)

One component of *personal income* estimates from the Bureau of Economic Analysis. Includes 1) wages and salaries paid to employees, 2) other labor income consisting primarily of employer contributions to private pension and welfare funds, and 3) income to self-employed individuals (proprietors), partnerships, and tax-exempt cooperatives.

labor force

The part of the population that is employed or available for work. The labor force includes people who are in the armed forces, employed, unemployed, or actively seeking employment. The Bureau of the Census currently publishes labor force statistics for persons age 16 years and older.

labor force participation rate

Proportion of people age 16 years and older who are in the *labor force*, that is, the number of people who are employed or available for work divided by the number of people who are age 16 years and older.

longitudinal study

A study that involves data collection from the same respondents at different points in time. For example, in a longitudinal study in Wisconsin, researchers interviewed a sample of farmers in 1982 and again in 1987 to learn how the respondents adjusted to major changes in the agricultural economy.

mean income

The average amount of income received, that is, *total income* divided by total population.

median income

The income level at which half of the population have lower incomes and half have higher incomes; the middle income level.

metropolitan (metro) county

The Census Bureau term for any county in a *metropolitan statistical area*.

metropolitan statistical area (MSA)

An area designated by the Census that is made up of one or more counties around a large population center, together with adjacent communities that are socially and economically integrated with the central city. An MSA must either have (a) a city with a population of at least 50,000 or (b) an urbanized area (which is a *census designated place*) with a population of at least 50,000 *and* a total MSA population of at least 100,000.

minor civil division (MCD)

The Census Bureau term for a governmental unit that is smaller than a county, such as a town or township.

money income

Term used by the Census Bureau for cash income such as wages and salaries, interest, rental income, Social Security payments, and public assistance.

occupation

Kind of work; a person's activity on the job either for pay or profit, such as farmer, nurse, computer programmer, bus driver, or logger.

natural increase

The difference between the number of births and deaths in a particular area. Together, natural increase and *net migration* are responsible for population change. (In rare instances, deaths outnumber births, resulting in natural decrease.)

net migration

The difference between the number of people who move into an area (in-migrants) and the number who move out (out-migrants). If in-migrants outnumber out-migrants, the area experiences net in-migration and vice versa.

nonmetropolitan (nonmetro) county

A county that is not part of a Census-designated *metropolitan statistical area.*

per capita income

The mean or average income received by individuals, that is, *total income* divided by the total number of people.

personal income

A measure of income used by the Bureau of Economic Analysis, defined as the income received by, or on behalf of, residents of a particular area. Includes *labor and proprietor income* less contributions for social insurance programs such as Social Security; dividends, interest, and rent; and transfer payments.

policy impact coding system

Classifies all *nonmetro* counties according to their economic base, the presence of federally owned land, and population characteristics (including retirement and persistently poor).

poverty level or threshold

An income level below which a family, household, or individual is officially considered to be poor. Each year, the U.S. Office of Management and Budget establishes a series of poverty income levels for different family sizes and ages of household heads. For example, in 1989, the poverty level for a family of four was $12,100.

poverty rate

The proportion of people living below the poverty level, that is, the number of people (individuals, families, or households) who have incomes less than the poverty level divided by the total population.

primary data

Collected by a researcher for a specific study, using for example, personal or telephone interviews.

proprietor income

A term used by the Bureau of Economic Analysis to refer to income received by proprietors (self-employed persons), persons in business partnerships, and members of tax-exempt cooperatives.

real dollars

Current dollars that have been adjusted by the *consumer price index* to reflect inflation (or deflation). Economists adjust current dollars so they can measure the dollars' value in terms of the goods and services that can be purchased. Hence, 1989 income measured in *real* terms (for example) can be compared to 1970 income because the effect of inflation has been removed. *Current dollars* divided by the *consumer price index* equal real dollars.

quintile

A group that makes up one-fifth of the distribution of a given population. With respect to income, the lowest quintile of families has the characteristic that four-fifths of all other families in the population have higher incomes.

rural

A term used to describe all persons (or areas) that are not designated by the Census as *urban*.

sample design

The method used to select a sample of elements from a given population for purposes of analysis. Examples of sample designs are (1) *random sampling*, where a scientifically generated table of random numbers is used to select elements, and (2) *systematic sampling*, where every *k*th (for example, every 10th or 50th) element of the population is selected for analysis.

sampling rate or ratio

The proportion of elements in a population that is selected for analysis.

secondary data

Existing data that have already been collected and transferred to hard copy, microfiche, or a computer accessible format. Examples of secondary data sources are the *County and City Data Book* and reports from the decennial census.

service industry

Includes establishments that provide services to individuals, businesses, and governments. These are personal services, private household services, miscellaneous business and repair services, amusement and recreation services, professional, social, and related services, and hotels and other lodging places.

service sector

Includes all industries that produce no tangible product, such as transportation, communications, trade, establishments in the *service industry*, and government.

standard industrial classification (SIC) system

The Federal government's method of grouping businesses and other establishments by the type of economic activity in which they are engaged.

survey data

Data collected with a questionnaire for specific research rather than in the course of an organization's normal business. Decennial census data are survey data.

time series data

Observations on the same unit (for example, on the per acre price of Iowa cropland or on median household income) at more than one (usually many) points in time.

total personal income

Summary income measure from the Bureau of Economic Analysis that includes all income received by persons in a given area. See *personal income*.

transfer payments

Income received not in return for current services, for example, Unemployment Insurance, Social Security, Aid to Families with Dependent Children, and Medicare.

unearned income

Income from the ownership of property and other assets (that is, dividends, interest, and rent) plus *transfer payments*.

urban

Term used by the Census Bureau to describe the population of all persons living in *urbanized areas* as well as persons living in places of 2,500 or more inhabitants outside *urbanized areas*.

urbanized area

Central cities and surrounding densely settled territory with a combined population of at least 50,000 inhabitants.

wage and salary income

Income earned at a job. The "labor" component of *labor and proprietor income*.

APPENDICES

Appendix A   Selected Data Series from the Bureau of the Census, U.S. Department of Commerce

Series and/or Title	Description	Frequency	Format[a]	Comments
POPULATION, CENSUS No. of Inhabitants (PC-1-A) General Pop. Char. (PC-1-B) General Soc. and Econ. Char. (PC-1-C).	Complete count and/or sample of items including demographic characteristics, education and labor force status, income by type and poverty status, urban/rural and metro/nonmetro breaks. Please see Census Catalog and Guide 1988, p. 9 for more detail.	Years ending in "0"	Published, fiche	1-A and B are available for MCDs, CCDs, county subdivisions and places. 1-C is available for places with pop. of 2,500 or more. Easy to use and available in local libraries.
HOUSING, CENSUS General Housing Char. (HC-1-A)	Complete count of items including number of units, number of rooms and occupants, and value. Urban/ rural and metro/nonmetro breaks.	Years ending in "0"	Published, fiche	Data for county subdivisions— places with at least 1,000 pop. Frequently available in public libraries.
POPULATION, CURRENT PROGRAMS Population Characteristics,[b] P-20	Marital status, household, and family characteristics, mobility, fertility, educational attainment, etc. Some metro/nonmetro classifications.	Annual	Published, fiche, on-line	Geographical detail below national level varies.
Special Studies,[b] P-23	Various subjects, including blacks, youth, women, older people, metro/nonmetro residents.	Irregular	Published, fiche, on-line	Geographical detail below national level varies.
Local Population Estimates, P-26	Estimates of population, components of change, and per capita income.	Irregular	Published, fiche, on-line, diskette	Estimates are made for counties and, in some cases, subcounty areas. Prepared jointly by state agencies and Census. Reliability of small place estimates is questionable.
Farm Population,[b] P-27	Age, race, and employment characteristics of the farm population.	Annual	Published, fiche	Only available for the U.S. and regions but useful for measuring changes in the farm population.
Consumer Income,[b] P-60	Money income, noncash benefits, and poverty status by demographic characteristics. Some metro/nonmetro classifications.	Annual	Published, fiche, on-line	National and regional.
AGRICULTURE, CENSUS Geographic Area Series (AC-A)	Number and characteristics of farms and farm operators, land in farms, value of products sold, etc.	Years ending in "2" and "7"	Published, fiche, on-line	Data are available at county level.
RETAIL TRADE, CENSUS Geographic Area Series (RC-A)	Number of establishments, employment, payroll, sales, etc., by various retail classifications.	Years ending in "2" and "7"	Published, fiche, on-line	Counties and cities with 500+ establishments, counties and cities with 2,500+ population.
WHOLESALE TRADE, CENSUS Geographic Area Seres (WC-A)	Number of establishments, employment, payroll, sales, etc.	Years ending in "2" and "7"	Published, fiche, on-line	Counties and cities with 200+ establishments, counties and cities with 2,500+ population.

Series and/or Title	Description	Frequency	Format[a]	Comments
SERVICE INDUSTRIES, CENSUS Geographic Area Series (SC-A)	Number of establishments, receipts, payroll, and employment by type of business.	Years ending in "2" and "7"	Published, fiche, on-line	Counties and cities with 750+ establishments, counties and cities with 2,500+ population.
MINERAL INDUSTRIES, CENSUS Geographic Area Series (MIC-A)	Value of shipments, value added by mining, employment, payroll, hours worked, etc., by SIC.	Years ending in "2" and "7"	Published, fiche, on-line	Counties
COUNTY BUSINESS PATTERNS	Number of employees in mid-March pay period, total payrolls, number and employment size class of establishments by 4-digit SIC, county. Federal employment and payroll for most states.	Annual	Published, fiche, diskette	Counties. Excludes farm and some other workers, also farmers and other self-employed.
GOVERNMENTS, CENSUS Governmental Organization (GC(1))	Local governments by type, size, and population; school systems by enrollment, etc.	Years ending in "2" and "7"	Published, fiche, on-line	Counties, municipalities, townships, school districts, special districts.
Taxable Property Values and Assessment-Sales Price Ratios (GC(2))	Assessed valuations, measurable sales, number of properties, etc.	Years ending in "2" and "7"	Published, fiche, on-line	Counties and cities of 50,000+ population.
Government Employment (GC(3))	Public employees, payrolls, October earnings, employment by function, etc.	Years ending in "2" and "7"	Published, fiche, on-line	Type of government, counties.
Government Finances (GC(4))	Revenue by source and type, expenditures, debt information, etc.	Years ending in "2" and "7"	Published, fiche, on-line	Type of government, counties.
GOVERNMENTS, SURVEY Government Employment (GE)	Employment and payroll.	Annual	Published, fiche	By size classification of counties, cities, townships.
Government Finances (GF)	Federal, state, and local finances.	Annual	Published, fiche, on-line	By size classification of counties and selected subcounty areas.
Quarterly Summary of Federal, State, and Local Tax Revenue (GT)	Revenue by level of government and type of tax, county property tax collections.	Quarterly	Published, fiche	By size classification of counties.
Consolidated Federal Funds Report	Grants, salaries and wages, procurement contracts, direct payments to individuals, other major programs.	Fiscal year	Published, fiche	Counties, municipalities, and townships (incorporated places only).
COUNTY AND CITY DATA BOOK	Statistical abstract supplement; data compiled from censuses, other agencies, and private sources. Population totals, income, education, etc.	Periodic	Published, fiche, on-line, diskette	Counties, incorporated places with 25,000+ population and places with 2,500+ population.

[a]May also be issued on tape
[b]From Current Population Survey

Source: U.S. Department of Commerce, Bureau of the Census (34)

Appendix B   Selected Items Collected and Published in the 1987 Economic Censuses for Counties[a]

Item	Retail Trade	Wholesale Trade	Service Industries	Manufac-turers	Mineral Industries
Number of Establishments and Firms					
Establishments with payroll	●	●	●[b]	●	●
Establishments without payroll[c]	●		●		
Establishments by legal form of organization	●		●		
Employment					
All employees	●	●	●	●	●
Production workers				●	●
Employment size of establishments				●	●
Production worker hours				●	●
Payroll					
All employees, entire year	●	●	●	●	●
All employees, first quarter	●	●	●		
Production workers				●	●
Sales, Receipts, or Value of Shipments					
For establishments with payroll	●	●	●[b]	●	●
For establishments without payroll	●		●		
Operating Expenses					
Value added				●	●
Capital expenditures, total				●	●

[a]Some data are also available for places with 2,500 inhabitants or more

[b]Subject to Federal income tax

[c]"Nonemployers," that is, businesses which do not employ any workers

Source: U.S. Department of Commerce, Bureau of the Census (47)

Appendix C   Regional Rural Development Centers

North Central Regional Center
  for Rural Development
Iowa State University
578 Heady Hall
Ames, Iowa 50011
Director: Peter Korsching
Phone: (515) 294-8322

North East Regional Center
  for Rural Development
Pennsylvania State University
104 Weaver Building
University Park, Pennsylvania 16802
Director: Daryl Heasley
Phone: (814) 863-4656

Southern Rural Development Center
P.O. Box 5446
Mississippi State, Mississippi 39762
Director: Doss Brodnax
Phone: (601) 325-3207

Western Rural Development Center
Oregon State University
Ballard Extension Hall 307
Corvallis, Oregon 97331-3601
Director: Russ Youmans
Phone: (503) 754-3621

Appendix D Depository Libraries, State Data Centers, and BLS Cooperating Agencies

State	Federal Depository Library [a]	State Data Center	BLS Cooperating State Agency
Alabama	Auburn University at Montgomery Library	Center for Business & Economic Research University of Alabama Tuscaloosa (205) 348-6191	Research and Statistics Alabama Dept. of Industrial Relations Montgomery (205) 261-5461
Alaska	Alaska State Library Juneau	Alaska State Data Center Department of Labor Juneau (907) 465-4500	Research and Analysis Section Alaska Department of Labor Juneau (907) 465-4500
Arizona	Dept. of Library Archives and Public Records	Arizona Department of Economic Security Phoenix (602) 255-5984	Research Administrator Arizona Department of Economic Security Phoenix (602) 255-3616
Arkansas	Arkansas State Library Little Rock	State Data Center University of Arkansas - Little Rock Little Rock (501) 371-1973	Research & Statistics Section ES Division, Arkansas Department of Labor Little Rock (501) 682-3194
California	California State Library Sacramento	State Census Data Center Department of Finance Sacramento (916) 322-4651	Employment Development Department Employment Data & Research Division Sacramento (916) 427-4675
Colorado	Denver Public Library Denver	Division of Local Government Colorado Department of Local Affairs Denver (303) 866-2156	Labor Market Information Colorado Division of Labor & Employment Denver (303) 620-6316
Connecticut	Connecticut State Library Hartford	Comprehensive Planning Division CT Office of Policy & Management Hartford (203) 566-8285	Res. & Info., Employment Security Division Connecticut Department of Labor Wethersfield (203) 566-2120
Delaware	Delaware State College Dover	Delaware Development Office Dover (302) 736-4271	Off. of Occupational & Labor Market Info. Delaware Department of Labor Newark (302) 368-6962

State	Federal Depository Library [a]	State Data Center	BLS Cooperating State Agency
District of Columbia	Department of Commerce Library	Data Services Division Mayor's Office of Planning Washington (202) 727-6533	Labor Market Information & Analysis D.C. Department of Employment Services Washington (202) 639-1642
Florida	University of Florida Libraries Gainesville	Florida State Data Center Office of Planning & Budgeting Tallahassee (904) 487-2814	Bureau of Labor Market Information FL Dept. of Labor & Employment Security Tallahassee (904) 488-1048
Georgia	University of Georgia Libraries Athens	Div. of Demographic & Stat. Services Georgia Office of Planning Budget Atlanta (404) 656-0911	Labor Information Systems Georgia Department of Labor Atlanta (404) 656-3177
Guam	Robert F. Kennedy Memorial Library	Guam Department of Commerce Tamuning (671) 646-5841	
Hawaii	University of Hawaii Library Honolulu	Hawaii State Data Center State Dept. of Business Economic Dev. Honolulu (808) 548-3082	Research & Statistics Office Dept. of Labor & Industrial Relations Honolulu (808) 548-7639
Idaho	University of Idaho Library Moscow	Idaho Department of Commerce Boise (208) 334-4714	Research & Analysis Idaho Department of Employment Boise (208) 334-6169
Illinois	Illinois State Library Springfield	Division of Planning & Financial Analysis Illinois Bureau of the Budget Springfield (217) 782-1381	Office of Economic Information & Analysis Illinois Department of Employment Security Chicago (312) 793-2316
Indiana	Indiana State Library Indianapolis	Indiana State Library Indiana State Data Center Indianapolis (317) 232-3735	LMI and Statistical Service IN Dept. of Employment & Training Services Indianapolis (317) 232-7701
Iowa	University of Iowa Libraries Iowa City	Census Services Iowa State University Ames (515) 294-8337	Audit and Analysis Iowa Department of Employment Services Des Moines (515) 281-8181

State	Federal Depository Library [a]	State Data Center	BLS Cooperating State Agency
Kansas	Watson Library Lawrence	State Library Topeka (913) 296-3296	Research & Analysis Kansas Department of Human Resources Topeka (913) 296-5061
Kentucky	University of Kentucky Libraries Lexington	Urban Studies Center University of Louisville (502) 588-7990	Labor Market Research & Analysis Department for Employment Services Frankfort (502) 564-7976
Louisiana	LA State Univ.: Middleton Library Baton Rouge	Louisiana State Planning Office Division of Administration Baton Rouge (504) 342-7410	Louisiana Department of Labor Baton Rouge (504) 342-3140
Maine	Univ. of ME, Raymond Fogler Libr. Orono	Division of Economic Analysis & Research Maine Department of Labor Augusta (207) 289-2271	Division of Economic Analysis & Research Maine Bureau of Employment Security Augusta (207) 289-2271
Maryland	University of MD, McKeldin Library College Park	Maryland Department of State Planning Baltimore (301) 225-4450	Research & Analysis Division Maryland Dept. of Employment & Training Baltimore (301) 333-5000
Massachusetts	Boston Public Library Boston	MA Inst. for Social & Economic Research University of Massachusetts Amherst (413) 545-0176	MA Department of Employment & Training Boston (617) 727-6556
Michigan	Michigan State Library Lansing	Michigan Information Center Department of Management & Budget Lansing (517) 373-2697	Research & Statistics Division Michigan Employment Security Commission Detroit (313) 876-5445
Minnesota	Univ. of Minnesota: Wilson Library Minneapolis	State Demographic Unit Minnesota State Planning Agency St. Paul (612) 296-4886	Research & Statistics Division Minnesota Department of Jobs & Training St. Paul (612) 296-6545
Mississippi	University of Mississippi Library University	Center for Population Studies The University of Mississippi University (601) 232-7288	Labor Market Information Division Mississippi Employment Security Comm. Jackson (601) 961-7976

State	Federal Depository Library [a]	State Data Center	BLS Cooperating State Agency
Missouri	Missouri State Library Jefferson City	Missouri State Library Jefferson City (314) 751-3615	Research and Analysis Missouri Division of Employment Security Jefferson City (314) 751-3591
Montana	Univ. of Montana, Mansfield Library Missoula	Census and Economic Info. Montana Department of Commerce Helena (406) 444-2896	Center Research and Analysis Department of Labor & Industry Helena (406) 449-2430
Nebraska	Nebraska Library Lincoln	Commission Bureau of Business Research The University of Nebraska-Lincoln Lincoln (402) 472-2334	Labor Market Information Nebraska Department of Labor Lincoln (402) 475-8451
Nevada	University of Nevada Library Reno	Nevada State Library Capitol Complex Carson City (702) 271-2155	Employment Security Research Nevada Employment Security Department Carson City (702) 885-4550
New Hampshire	New Hampshire State Library Concord	Office of State Planning Concord (603) 271-2155	Economic Analysis and Reports NH Department of Employment Security Concord (603) 228-4123
New Jersey	Newark Public Library Newark	New Jersey Department of Labor Division of Planning & Research Trenton (609) 984-2593	Division of Planning and Research New Jersey Department of Labor Trenton (609) 292-2643
New Mexico	New Mexico State Library Santa Fe	Economic Development & Tourism Santa Fe (505) 827-0276	Dept. Employment Security Comm. of NM Tiwa Building Albuquerque (505) 841-8638
New York	New York State Library Albany	NY State Dept. of Econ. Development Albany (518) 474-6005	Division of Research & Statistics New York State Department of Labor Albany (518) 457-6181
North Carolina	U of NC at Chapel Hill Library Chapel Hill	NC Office of State Budget & Mgmt. Raleigh (919) 733-7061	Labor Market Information Division Employment Security Commission of NC Raleigh (919) 733-2936

State	Federal Depository Library [a]	State Data Center	BLS Cooperating State Agency
North Dakota	ND State University Library Fargo	Department of Agricultural Economics North Dakota State University Fargo (701) 237-8621	Research and Statistics Job Service North Dakota Bismarck (701) 224-2825
Ohio	State Library of Ohio Columbus	Ohio Data Users Center Ohio Department of Development Columbus (614) 466-2115	Labor Market Information Division Ohio Bureau of Employment Services Columbus (614) 481-5783
Oklahoma	Oklahoma Department of Libraries Oklahoma City	Oklahoma State Data Center Oklahoma Department of Commerce Oklahoma City (405) 843-9770	Research and Planning Division Employment Security Commission Oklahoma City (405) 557-7110
Oregon	Portland State Univ. Library Portland	Center for Population & Census Portland State University Portland (503) 229-3922	Research & Statistics Oregon Employment Division Salem (503) 378-3220
Pennsylvania	State Library of Pennsylvania Harrisburg	Pennsylvania State Data Center Institute for State & Regional Affairs Middletown (717) 948-6336	Research & Statistics Division PA Department of Labor & Industry Harrisburg (717) 787-3265
Puerto Rico	University of Puerto Rico Rio Piedras	Puerto Rico Planning Board Minillas Government Center San Juan (809) 728-4430	Department of Labor & Human Resources Bureau of Labor Statistics Hato Rey (809) 754-5339
Rhode Island	Rhode Island State Library Providence	RI Statewide Planning Program Providence (401) 277-2656	Employment Security Research RI Department of Employment Security Providence (401) 277-3704
South Carolina	South Carolina State Library Columbia	Division of Research & Stat. Services South Carolina Budget & Control Board Columbia (803) 734-3780	Labor Market Information Division SC Employment Security Commission Columbia (803) 737-2660
South Dakota	South Dakota State Library Pierre	Business Research Bureau University of South Dakota Vermillion (605) 677-5287	Labor Market Information Center Department of Labor Aberdeen (605) 622-2314

State	Federal Depository Library [a]	State Data Center	BLS Cooperating State Agency
Tennessee	TN State Library & Archives Nashville	Tennessee State Planning Office Nashville (615) 741-1676	Research & Statistics Division TN Department of Employment Security Nashville (615) 741-2284
Texas	Texas State Library Austin	State Data Center Texas Department of Commerce Austin (512) 472-5059	Texas Employment Commission Austin (512) 463-2858
Utah	Utah State U., Merrill Library Logan	Office of Planning & Budget Salt Lake City Utah (801) 533-6082	Labor Market Information Services Department of Employment Security Salt Lake City (801) 533-2014
Vermont	Vermont Department of Libraries Montpelier	Office of Policy Res. & Coordination Montpelier (802) 828-3326	Office of Policy & Public Information VT Department of Employment & Training Montpelier (802) 229-0311
Virginia	University of VA: Alderman Library Charlottesville	Virginia Employment Commission Richmond (804) 786-8624	Economic Information Services Virginia Employment Commission Richmond (804) 786-5670
Washington	Washington State Library Olympia	Estimation & Forecasting Unit Office of Financial Management Olympia (206) 586-2504	Labor Mkt. & Economic Analysis Branch WA Employment Security Department Olympia (206) 438-4800
West Virginia	West Virginia University Library Morgantown	Community Development Division Governor's Office of Comm. & Ind. Dev. Charleston (304) 348-4010	Division of Labor & Economic Security WV Department of Employment Security Charleston (304) 348-2660
Wisconsin	State Historical Society Library Madison	Demographic Services Center Department of Administration Madison (608) 266-1927	Division of Employment & Training Policy Dept. of Industry, Labor & Human Relations Madison (608) 266-5843
Wyoming	Wyoming State Library Cheyenne	Institute for Policy Research University of Wyoming Laramie (307) 766-5141	Research and Analysis Section Employment Security Commission Casper (307) 235-3646

[a] Other libraries in each state are also designated as Federal Depository Libraries. See Census Catalog and Guide for complete listing or call the depository library nearest you.

Appendix E Guide to the *CCDB* Files on Diskette

The *County and City Data Book 1988* (*CCDB*) diskette files make a wide variety of small area data available to any user with an IBM-compatible microcomputer. Although the diskettes do not offer more information than the printed report, they do make it easier to manipulate and to display the data. Because the Census Bureau provides an easy to use, menu-driven utility program with each order, using the files requires no supplemental software or technical skills. In addition, the Census Bureau staff people who developed the files are extremely helpful and go out of their way to make this particular product easy to use. Telephone inquiries are answered promptly.

Content

Census offers six file sets or packages of diskettes:

File Set 1. Counties (18 diskettes). 209 data items for the U.S., 50 states, District of Columbia, and 3,139 counties and county equivalents.

File Set 2. Cities (4 diskettes). 139 data items for the U.S., 50 states, District of Columbia, and 957 cities with 25,000 or more inhabitants in 1980.

File Set 3. Places (3 diskettes). 6 data items for the U.S., 50 states, District of Columbia, and incorporated places with 2,500 or more inhabitants in 1986.

File Set 4. States (1 diskette). All data items from the County, City, and Place files for the U.S., 50 states, and the District of Columbia.

File Set 5. Divisions (25 diskettes, available in 7 subsets). All data items from the County, City, and Place files for each census division and its states, counties, cities, and places.

File Set 6. Special Subjects (20 diskettes, available in 2 subsets). Data from County and City file sets. Subset 1 (9 diskettes) contains demographic data for all counties and cities. Subset 2 (11 diskettes) contains economic data for all counties and cities.

Sets 1, 5, and 6 contain county data. Set 1 is most inclusive because it covers all counties and all data items in the published report. Set 5 is most appropriate for users who are interested in a specific region. Set 6 is most appropriate for those interested in only one subject area.

Each diskette in Sets 1-3 contains only a pair of files: a data file (extension .TXT) and a dictionary file (extension .DCT).[1] In the County File Set, the data files are numbered COF01.TXT through COF18.TXT, while the dictionary files are numbered COF01.DCT through COF18.DCT.

Each data file consists of one record or string of data for every geographic area in the set. For example, COF01.TXT contains 3,191 records—one for the U.S., each state, the District of Columbia, and each county and county equivalent. Every record in COF01.TXT includes four data items that identify and describe the geographic area a FIPS code,[2] a geographic level code that denotes whether the record is for a state or county, an MSA code, and the area name. It also includes 10 data items. The first 4 identifier variables in each file (COF01.TXT through COF18.TXT) are identical; only the data items differ.

---

[1]Diskettes in sets 4-6 each contain individual extracts from the three geographic area files. Therefore, instead of having two files, they have six.
[2]Each county in the U.S. has a unique 5-digit FIPS (Federal Information Processing Standard) code. The sequential codes are assigned alphabetically. Hence, the FIPS code for Autauga County in Alabama is 01001. "01" is for Alabama, "001" is for Autauga County.

Each dictionary file contains one record (or string of descriptive information) for each field or data item in the data file.

Ordering the Files

Cost of the *CCDB 1988* files is:

File Set 1	$ 264
File Set 2	$ 96
File Set 3	$ 84
File Set 4	$ 60
File Set 5	$ 84 – 96/subset
File Set 6	$ 156 for subset 1, $ 180 for subset 2

The free technical documentation that accompanies each order explains how to use the diskettes. Also included with each order is a diskette containing an easy to use, menu-driven utility program that enables users to access, partition, and recombine the data.

Census offers a discount if more than one set is ordered. Subsets are available only for sets 5 and 6. Contact Customer Services (Order Desk), Bureau of the Census (301) 763-4100 for further information and order forms.

Using the Files

The *CCDB* files can be used with IBM compatible computers that have either two floppy disk drives or a hard disk. For purposes of describing how to use the files, we assume that readers have two floppy disk drives designated A and B and that they have ordered the County file set. The County file set contains a total of 36 files: 18 data files with the extension ".TXT" and 18 dictionary files with the extension ".DCT"

The steps in using the files are as follows:

1. Make back-up copies of all diskettes included in the order and read the Appendix called "UTILITY2 Program Documentation."

2. Insert the utility diskette in Drive A and one of the data diskettes in Drive B.

3. Type in "UTILITY2" and hit RETURN. The master menu will appear on the screen. Follow the directions on page A-2 of "UTILITY2 Program Documentation.

From the master menu, users can look at data from a file on the screen, produce a custom designed hard copy of the data, create a subset of data records and/or of data items, and string records from several files together. It is also possible to create an output file that can be loaded into LOTUS 1-2-3™. The documentation describes each of these alternatives in detail.

INDEX